CHRONOLOGY OF FIFA WORLD CUP 2018

Chronology of FIFA World Cup 2018
by Gunnmay Marwaha
Second Paperback Edition

First Edition Published in 2018 by Gunnmay Marwaha
Second Edition Published in 2023 in India by

Inkfeathers

Inkfeathers Publishing
Vivek Vihar, New Delhi 110 095
www.inkfeathers.com

ISBN 978-81-19483-51-8

CHRONOLOGY OF FIFA WORLD CUP 2018

GUNNMAY MARWAHA

Inkfeathers Publishing
www.inkfeathers.com

DEDICATION

To the luminous constellations gracing the pitch with their extraordinary brilliance, this book is dedicated. To the unyielding spirit of those who dance with the ball, weaving dreams with every step, this tribute is etched. Each superstar, a brushstroke in the masterpiece of football's history, has painted the canvas of our hearts with unforgettable moments.

From the soaring heights of victory to the humbling lessons of defeat, you have shown us the embodiment of dedication, teamwork, and sheer artistry. With every thunderous goal, elegant pass, and daring dribble, you've woven a tapestry of emotions that transcends borders and cultures.

This dedication echoes through the stadiums that have witnessed your magic and resounds in the cheers of millions. You've become the icons of a sport that unites the world, proving that a single ball can carry the dreams of many.

To the superstars of football, past and present, this book is a tribute to your eternal glow on and off the pitch.

DEDICATION

GOLDEN TESTIMONIAL

Coach Micheal Bassey, Head Coach, India on Track

"It was a beautiful afternoon during my first soccer class at Manav Rachna Sports Academy in collaboration with India on Track (IOT). During our first training session, I observed a little boy named Gunnmay Marwaha, his passion for football was written all over his face. Technically, he could not have been compared with other kids who could receive and pass the ball properly, but he was keen to learn. I remember the sadness on his face after the session; on that day, he was not happy; I called him to ask why he was sad, and he told me he could not play football well and was not getting the ball from his teammates. I do remember telling him that he needs to believe in himself, that he should enjoy the game and, at the same time, pay attention to the coach, and that he would improve with time. The passionate little Gunnmay followed that instruction, and from the next soccer class, Gunnmay consistently reported on time for most of the classes before other kids would arrive. He takes out one ball and practices all alone before the session begins. Today I can tell you that after a year, Gunnmay can receive the ball very well and shoot with both feet.

His love for the game is unbelievable. Gunnmay went on to receive the highest certificate for the most attended soccer classes of the month. He is very knowledgeable about the game of football. He keeps track of every event happening around the world of football. As his coach, I will say Gunnmay dreams of football, eats and thinks about football. With determination and hard work, anything is achievable. Keep moving, Gunnmay; the sky is your limit."

PRAISE FOR THE BOOK

Sports Enthusiast–Soccer Star

Not only is Gunnmay intellectually gifted, but he also excels in the world of sports, particularly soccer. His agility, speed, and precision on the soccer field have earned them recognition as a budding soccer star. has been a valuable team player, consistently contributing to his team's success while impressing coaches and teammates with his skills. He fell in love with soccer at the age of four and quickly rose through the ranks of his local youth team. It is this love of his for the beautiful game which he combines with his writing skills that he showcases to present the detailed and highlighted Chronology of FIFA World Cup 2018.

This book is a must buy for early enthusiasts and mature soccer fans. It provides for good coffee table discussions. Surely an inspiration to peers and adults alike, Gunnmay's accomplishments at such a young age are nothing short of remarkable.

Col. Dr. C.S. Pant, V.S.M.

"If you have a scream in your goal announcement, an amazing youngster is blessing your place. Gunnmay has been a child with an amazing love of football and has the amazing capacity to write up the records."

Eric Benjamin - Xtelcos FC

"A passionate compilation of all major talk-worthy points by a definitive lover of the beautiful game. Soccer has been blessed for generations since it breeds such amazing young followers. Extremely inspiring effort. Do not miss at all."

Rahul Saini, Regional Sportsperson and Critic

"What an amazing chronology. It has everything that we want to remember about FIFA World Cup 2018. All the juice is very well documented in the thrilling pages. Worthy of a library edition. A must-have coffee table book."

AUTHOR'S NOTE

Dear Reader and Fan,

As I set out to write this book on the beautiful game of soccer, I am filled with a sense of passion and nostalgia that has been a constant companion throughout my journey from learning, playing and writing about soccer. Soccer, to me, is not just a sport; it is a source of inspiration, camaraderie, and unending fascination. It is a language spoken by millions, transcending borders, cultures, and backgrounds. It is a game that brings people together in celebration of skill, teamwork, and the pursuit of excellence. I am thrilled to present this book to you, a passionate exploration of the beautiful game that is soccer. As a lifelong enthusiast and an avid player myself, I have poured my heart and soul into crafting this. Whether you are a seasoned aficionado, a budding talent on the pitch, or simply someone curious about the sport, I hope this book provides you with a deeper understanding and appreciation for the world's most popular game.

As I sit down to write this author's note for my book on soccer, I am filled with gratitude and excitement. Soccer, often referred to as the beautiful game, has been an integral part of my life for as long as I can remember. It has shaped my childhood, influenced my friendships, and even played a role in my behaviour. In the pages that follow, I hope to convey the deep love I have for soccer and share the stories, insights, and experiences that have shaped my understanding of this sport.

Whether you are a lifelong devotee of the game, a curious newcomer, or somewhere in between, I aim to provide you with a journey through the world of soccer that is both informative and entertaining.

This book will not only explore the history and evolution of soccer but also delve into the artistry of the players, the strategies of the coaches, and the unwavering passion of the fans. We will venture into the highs and lows of the tournament—FIFA World Cup Russia. From the thrill of victory to the agony of defeat, and examine the profound impact it has had on societies around the globe, soccer is more than just a game played on a field; it is a reflection of the human spirit. It teaches us about dedication, perseverance, and the ability to overcome adversity. It shows us the power of unity and the beauty of individual brilliance. It reminds us that no matter where we come from, we can connect through a shared love for the sport.

So, whether you are reading this book as a player looking to improve your knowledge, a fan seeking a deeper understanding of the game, or simply someone who appreciates the beauty of soccer, I hope you find this book to be a valuable companion on your own soccer journey. Let us celebrate the world's most popular sport together and revel in the magic of soccer.

This book is not just about the technical aspects of the game or the statistics of the great players. It's about the stories, the emotions, and the experiences that make soccer unforgettable. From the heart-stopping drama of World Cup finals to the underdog triumphs in local leagues, every match tells a unique tale in this specific World Cup soccer. It's about the dedicated coaches who mould young talents, the tireless volunteers who maintain the grassroots of the sport, and the fans whose unwavering support transforms stadiums into electrifying cauldrons of excitement.

I invite you to embark on this journey with me, as we delve into the history, tactics, and human stories that make soccer the global phenomenon it is today. Whether you're reading this book for the love of the game or to deepen your knowledge, I hope you find inspiration and a renewed sense of wonder in every page.

Thank you for joining me on this incredible adventure through the world of soccer. May the spirit of the game continue to unite us all, and may its magic never fade.

Gunnmay Marwaha

FOREWORD

It is a pleasure indeed to introduce to all an amazing showcase of the highlights of FIFA World Cup 2018, Russia. This tournament is dubbed to be not just the premier event of the beautiful game but rather the largest sporting event on this planet alongside the likes of the Olympics.

The United Nations Organisation today has 193 registered member countries. At the same time, FIFA boasts 211 member associations, making it the "United Nations of Football."

The chronology that follows is an extremely well-laid highlight chain of events spiced with pictures, notable figures, results of matches, the event venues, and high and quotable points taken from newspaper articles and cuttings, making this an indispensable library fixture for any football fan. Being an "8-year old's" work, it is a sure contest to several expert's collations, exhibiting massive diligence and passion.

Proud of you, Gunnmay!

Gaurav Marwaha

FIFA RUSSIA WORLD CUP 2018

LIST OF QUALIFIED TEAMS

UEFA (EUROPE)s

Qualified: Russia (host), Belgium, Germany, England, Spain, Poland, Iceland, Serbia, France, Portugal, Switzerland, Croatia, Sweden, Denmark

Recently Eliminated: Czech Republic, Norway, Israel, Hungary, Turkey, Ukraine, Netherlands, Greece, Italy, Ireland

A.F.C. (A.S.I.A.)

Qualified: Iran, South Korea, Japan, Saudi Arabia, Australia

Recently Eliminated: Uzbekistan, China, United Arab Emirates, Iraq, Thailand, Qatar, Syria

C.A.F. (A.F.R.I.C.A.)

Qualified: Nigeria, Egypt, Senegal, Tunisia, Morocco

Recently Eliminated: Cameroon, Algeria, Guinea, Libya, Congo, Zambia, Uganda, Ghana, South Africa

CONCACAF (NORTH AMERICA)

Qualified: Mexico, Costa Rica, Panama

Recently Eliminated: United States, Canada, El Salvador, Trinidad & Tobago, Haiti, Jamaica, Guatemala

CONMEBOL (SOUTH AMERICA)

Qualified: Brazil, Uruguay, Argentina, Colombia, Peru

Recently Eliminated: Bolivia, Venezuela, Ecuador, Chile, Paraguay

OFC (OCEANIA)

Qualified: None

Recently Eliminated: New Zealand, Solomon Islands, Fiji, New Caledonia, Tahiti, Papua New Guinea.

The 21st FIFA Russia World Cup will commence on the 14th of June.

Eight different nations have won the 20 World Cup tournaments. Brazil has won the most titles, five. The current champion is Germany, who won the title in 2014.

Brazil 5: 1958, 1962, 1970, 1994, 2002

Germany 4: 1954, 1974, 1990, 2014

Italy 4: 1934, 1938, 1982, 2006

Argentina 2: 1978, 1986

Uruguay 2: 1930, 1950

England 1: 1966

France 1: 1998

Spain 1: 2010

NEWS (BEFORE THE FIFA WORLD CUP RUSSIA 2018)

9 DAYS TO GO

Neymar is only at 80%

Brazil star Neymar said he was very happy to have made a goal-scoring comeback in a 2-0 friendly victory over Croatia but insisted he was only firing at 80 per cent. "It's been three months since I've been injured. To come back and do what I love most, playing football, and scoring a goal, is an immense joy. I'm very happy." He added, "I still feel a little pain, but that's normal when you spend most of your time not walking. I feel at 80 per cent of my capacity."

Mo Salah Injured

Liverpool striker Mohamed Salah was included in Egypt's 2018 World Cup squad despite still undergoing treatment for a shoulder injury that he suffered in the Champions League final; the Egyptian Football Association said, "Salah has undergone treatment in Valencia, Spain, in the hope of playing a role in Egypt's first appearance in the World Cup since 1990. The federation said Salah would be out for not more than three weeks, meaning he could miss Egypt's opening World Cup group A fixture against Uruguay.

Paolo Guerrero Returns to Action

Paolo Guerrero scored twice in a 3-0 friendly win over Saudi Arabia to cap an emotional week for the Peru captain, who has been cleared to play at the World Cup after his long legal battle against a 14-month drugs suspension. Guerrero has played just a handful of matches for his Brazilian club Flamengo since he was initially banned on the 3rd of November, a ruling that forced him out of Peru's two-legged World Cup play-off against New Zealand. His two goals sealed the win after Andre Carrillo fired the South Americans ahead on 21 min. Apart from the 34-year-old icon, the team will need a spark from another veteran attacker, Jefferson Farfan.

Kompany Injured

Belgium coach Roberto Martinez has given Vincent Kompany two weeks to recover from a groin injury in time for the World Cup, retaining the Manchester City captain in his squad but putting Laurent Ciman on standby for the tournament in Russia. Coach Roberto Martinez named a 24-man squad. For now, the players cut are goalkeeper Matz Sels, defenders Christian Kabasele and Jordan Lukaku, and striker Christian Benteke.

8 DAYS TO GO

Mastercard New Campaign

MasterCard said it was changing a campaign in which thousands of meals were given to the needy every time Neymar and Messi scored goals. Under the scheme, every time the duo scored, 10,000 meals would be donated to the United Nations World Food Programme. The idea drew fire across social media, and Brazilian coach Tite also criticised it as counterproductive as it put too much pressure on individual stars." We don't want the fans, players, or anyone else to lose focus of the crucial question of hunger and our efforts to help this cause." said MasterCard.

Messi Doesn't Consider Himself the Best

Barcelona star striker Lionel Messi has refused to consider himself the world's best player and dubbed himself as 'just another player' as the Argentinian prepares for the World Cup. Despite winning nine La Liga titles, four Champions League crowns, five Ballon d'Or, and 552 goals for Barcelona, Messi insisted that every player is the same when on the field "I don't consider myself as the best player; I think I'm just another. On the field, we are all the same when the game begins," Messi said. At the World Cup, Messi said, "It will be important to prepare well because, in the qualifiers, we were fighting up to the end, and we didn't have time to prepare." He said, "We still have time to make ourselves stronger to be at the same level as other teams like Spain, Germany, Brazil, or Belgium.

Spanish Squad Has a Busy Day

The Spanish squad had a busy Tuesday as they were visited by the new Spanish prime minister Pedro Sanchez, posed for their official team photo, and underwent dope tests. Sanchez handed Andres Iniesta the medal 'Cross of Sporting Merit.' Sanchez said, "Everyone remembers your World Cup-winning goal in Johannesburg and who we were with when we celebrated." Captain Sergio Ramos spoke on the Mo Salah controversy." Everything gets blown out of context, but he holds onto me; I fell the other way, and he hurt his arm, and people said I used a judo throw on him. Then Karius suffered a concussion after a collision with me; all it needs is Firminho to say he caught a cold after a drop of my sweat fell on him."

Keralite Gets Included in the Saudi World Cup Squad.

Trust the World Cup to help highlight the inclusion of the Keralite Diaspora in Saudi Arabian society. The largest Indian ethnic group in the Gulf country got a pleasant surprise. When an official online video by the Saudi Arabian Football Federation announcing their World Cup squad showed citizens joyous reactions as each player's name came up in the video through TV news or radio announcement, or mobile phone alerts. Towards the end of the video, Malayalam makes a cameo appearance. A Keralite can be seen seated in a barber shop, eyes shut as shaving cream is applied on his face when the radio blurts out in Malayalam, "Do you know Abdul Malik Akhbairi has been included in the Saudi Arabian squad for the World Cup" Then opens his eyes and looks at the barber with a huge smile on his face clearly, he is overjoyed by Akhbairi's inclusion, that too in his native tongue. The presence of Malayalam in an official Saudi video gives it traction whilst acknowledging India's contribution to Saudi's economy.

7 DAYS TO GO

Home-based players

Every four years, the World Cup becomes a great big melting pot. Footballers from every corner of the world meet for a month-long festival. How do the demographics of this congregation play out? With the official squads of the 32 teams announced, FIFA revealed that 736 footballers will be in Russia in 2018. According to a study by the European Club Association, European clubs will provide staggering 544 players in Russia—74% of the total. At the same time, Africa brings up the rear with 21.

Furthermore, the commercial success of the English Premiership is mirrored in the fact that all 23 of England's players are home based. Traditional footballer assembly lines, Brazil and Argentina, each have only three home-based players in their squads. Italian football continues to hold sway, even without qualifying. Italy's Serie A footballers are fourth on the list of most representations in Russia. England is the only team where all 23 players are home-based, while Senegal and Sweden have none. The following is the list of how many players are home-based from each country.

England - 23

Russia - 21

Saudi Arabia - 20

Spain - 19

Germany - 15

South Korea - 12

Iran and France - 9

Costa Rica and Portugal - 6

Tunisia and Peru - 5

Poland - 4

Argentina, Australia, Columbia, Brazil, Denmark,

Panama, and Serbia - 3

Croatia, Morocco, and Uruguay - 2

Egypt, Japan, and Mexico - I

Switzerland, Iceland, Nigeria, and Belgium - 1

Senegal and Sweden – 0

Palestinian Football terror

The Israeli and Palestinian football associations traded accusations over the cancellation of a World Cup warm-up match between the Jewish state and Argentina in the disputed city of Jerusalem. Israel accused the Palestinians of "football terror", saying their threats saw Lionel Messi and his team abandon what will be the final friendly before Russia. An unverified tweet quoting Messi rejecting to play the match was also doing the rounds on social media." As a UNICEF ambassador, I cannot play against people who kill innocent Palestinian children. We had to cancel the as we were humans before footballers." the tweet quoted Messi saying. The Palestinians, meanwhile, rejected the allegation, saying the Argentinians pulled out of the match as they realised that Israel was using their presence for political gain." They've finally done the right thing. Rationale and health come before everything else. We think it's best not to go to Israel." said the Argentinian striker Gonzalo Higuaín. The match was called off on Tuesday after a campaign by the Palestinians following its relocation to Jerusalem. "We are confronting a football terror from the Palestinian Football Association and its President (Jibril Rajoub)," said Rotem Kamer of the Israel Football Association. He accused them of threatening the players and their families. Palestinians hotly opposed the sold-out game in Jerusalem. It was originally scheduled to take place in Haifa but was moved to Jerusalem.

Brazilian Net Sold for Charity

One of the nets in Brazil's humiliating 2014 World Cup semi-final defeat against Germany will be cut up and sold for charity. The Mineirão stadium in Belo Horizonte, where Brazil's footballing meltdown occurred four years ago, announced the sale on Tuesday. The net will be cut into 8,150 pieces and sold online for a minimum of 71 Euros (about $83) a piece, the price echoing the infamous score line. One of the nets will remain in Belo Horizonte. Still, the one going to charity saw most of the action: a barrage of five German first-half goals and the solitary Brazilian goal in the second half. Organisers hope to raise at least 500,000 Euros ($586,000) for charities in Brazil.

Klose Defends Loew's Decision

Miroslav Klose defended Joachim Loew's decision to ignore Leroy Sane for his World Cup squad, saying the winger failed to take his chances. The decision to leave Leroy Sane out of Germany's World Cup squad was taken because he failed to impress when on international duty, according to Miroslav Klose. Sane enjoyed a remarkable season with Premier League winners Manchester City, scoring ten times and setting up another 15. Such impressive form resulted in him winning the Professional Footballers' Association (PFA.) Young Player of the Year award, while he was also nominated for the Players' Player of the Year. Yet, his consistent excellence at club level was not enough to convince Germany head coach Joachim Low and his support staff—which includes Klose—to look beyond his failings with the national team.

Although Klose recognises the 22-year-old's prodigious ability, he simply feels Sane did not do enough in training or matches to usurp Julian Brandt. "I said that we consulted with all coaches," Klose told reporters on Thursday. "He [Sane] knows that he is incredibly talented and brings a pace you don't see very often." He shows that in the Premier League, but to be honest, he had many situations in training and during the games where he couldn't establish himself as he did in the Premier League.

"I told you before; it was a hard decision. It was a decision for Julian [Brandt] and not against Leroy. It was really close."

Germany played their final World Cup preparation game against Saudi Arabia on Friday before getting their title defence underway in a clash with Mexico on the 17th of June.

Ozil Injured

Germany's final World Cup warm-up match takes place against Saudi Arabia on Friday. Still, Mesut Ozil will not feature due to a knee injury.

Mesut Ozil will miss his country's final World Cup preparation match against Saudi Arabia with a "minor" knee injury, the German Football Association (DFB) has confirmed.

Ozil scored Germany's goal in a 2-1 defeat to Austria on Saturday but has since struggled with a bruised knee.

It has been reported that the Arsenal man has missed four days of training as a result.

While some sections of the media have suggested Ozil is a doubt for Germany's World Cup opener against Mexico on the 17th of June, an announcement from the DFB stated his absence from Friday's game is simply "precautionary".

After facing Mexico, Germany will also play against Sweden and South Korea in Russia as they aim to defend their World Cup title.

Ronaldo Knows Portugal

Cristiano Ronaldo knows Portugal—who will face Spain, Morocco, and Iran at the World Cup—are not among the favourites in Russia.

Cristiano Ronaldo said Portugal must be realistic as they are not among the World Cup favourites. However, the Real Madrid superstar insisted nothing is impossible.

Euro 2016 champions Portugal will face Spain (on the 15th of June), Morocco (on the 19th of June), and Iran (on the 25th of June) in Group B at the World Cup in Russia.

Portugal defied the odds to be crowned European champions two years ago. Captain Ronaldo who is set to return to the starting XI for Thursday's friendly against Algeria, having enjoyed some rest following last month's Champions League triumph—said Fernando

Santos' men will give their all at the showpiece tournament.

Led by Ronaldo as Portugal was sent off to the World Cup at a Lisbon reception held by President Marcelo Rebello De Sousa Wednesday, the five-time Ballon d'Or winner said: "What I can guarantee is a great ambition of all of us players and technical team. "We know we are not the favourites; we have to be realistic, but in football, nothing is impossible." "I think we must think match by match. The first match, the group stage, will be extremely difficult, but I think that with these players, we need to think big, and I am confident that we will give our best."

"What I can say is that we will do the same [of Euro 2016] fight to the end, always keeping hope that in football everything is possible."

Ronaldo—Portugal's most capped player and leading scorer, continued. "Step by step, see what will happen, what the competition will bring us, and for us is a privilege to represent Portugal's colours [and] represent this nation. "We will give our best and wait to see what we will get from it. Thank you very much for having us here; us is a privilege; thank you very much."

Ronaldo is Poised to Return

Cristiano Ronaldo is poised to return as Portugal steps up their World Cup preparations with a warm-up fixture at home to Algeria. According to head coach Fernando Santos, Portugal captain Cristiano Ronaldo is set to be in the starting XI for Thursday's international friendly against Algeria. Ronaldo has been watching from the sidelines following Real Madrid's Champions League triumph last month—the five-time Ballon d'Or winner was absent for friendlies against Tunisia and Belgium.

However, the 33-year-old is poised to return as Euro 2016 champions Portugal step up their World Cup preparations with a warm-up fixture at home to Algeria. "Most likely, Cristiano will be in the starting line-up," Santos told reporters. "We will try to continue with the team's evolution, to analyse the last two matches and try to rectify some things because, after this, we have the first match against Spain, so it's important that the team can learn from these matches and from the last match too."

Of Ronaldo—Portugal's most capped player and record scorer—Santos added: "Any team in the world that has the best player in the world, he must have influence.

"At any team in the world, for any national squad or any club, to have Cristiano Ronaldo will always be very important for his team." Portugal will face Spain (on the 15th of June), Morocco (on the 19th of June), and Iran (on the 25th of June) in Group B at the World Cup in Russia.

Santos said he still has doubts about his line-up ahead of the showpiece tournament.

"I still have a lot of doubts, there are 23 players, but I have total confidence in all of them," he said. "The match against Spain will be in one week; we are going to see how the training sessions go and how the players are doing. I will decide at the right time; that conclusion can't be taken yet with the training sessions to come and any eventual thing that can happen. Of course, there's a basis [of players] that is defined, but I have full confidence in my 23 players, and that's the most important thing."

6 DAYS TO GO

Far From Ideal, says Santos.

Portugal head coach Fernando Santos said the European champions have plenty of room for improvement heading into the World Cup following their 3-0 win over Algeria.

Cristiano Ronaldo returned as Portugal prepared for the Russia showpiece with a routine victory against Algeria thanks to Goncalo Guedes' brace Thursday.

Guedes produced an eye-catching performance with goals either side of half-time to give Portugal a boost ahead of their Group B opener against Spain in Sochi on the 15th of June.

"We are still far from ideal; it is with the championship that we will grow," Santos said in Lisbon post-match. "There are some things to fine-tune; there are players playing together for the first time in this selection."

Paris Saint-Germain winger Guedes— who spent the season on loan at Valencia—upstaged Ronaldo in his 150th international appearance.

Bruno Fernando also opened his account for Portugal in the first half as Santos' men ended their three-match winless run.

"There were good things, but there are things to improve," Santos added. "In the first 20 or 25 minutes, the team was good, compact, and quick to react to the ball. If their strikers did not shine, it's a lot of merit for my team. We made a goal in that period, and we could have done more."

"Thereafter, we slowed down, but then we got back to normal, there were spaces to make goals, and we did." Santos continued: "You cannot draw any conclusions from this game. Obviously, we are getting closer to the starting XI. Still, the most important thing is to feel that I have 23 players prepared to compete."

GFA Dissolved

Ghana President Nana Akufo-Addo made the decision to dissolve the nation's football association amid fraud and corruption claims.

The country's government has dissolved Ghana's Football Association (GFA) amid allegations of corruption and bribery.

Nana Akufo-Addo—the President of Ghana—made the decision Thursday after footage emerged from a documentary allegedly uncovering fraud and corruption under the leadership of GFA boss Kwesi Nyantakyi.

In the documentary 'When Greed and Corruption Become the Norm', Nyantakyi was pictured accepting a cash gift from an undercover reporter who was pretending to be a businessman.

IS Poses a Threat the World Cup

The Islamic State (IS) poses a threat to the World Cup that must be taken seriously, security experts warn. Alarm bells have been ringing since disturbing photomontages began to appear on social media late last year. Crude and explicit, they showed stars such as Lionel Messi and Neymar dressed in orange suits used for videotaped executions. Lying on the ground with knives up to their throats or dying in flames, the message accompanying them was blunt. "You will not enjoy security until we live in it in Muslim countries," the posts said.

5 DAYS TO GO

Ronaldo's Back

With Cristiano Ronaldo back in the side, Portugal strolled to a 3-0 victory over Algeria in a warm-up match in Lisbon. A brace from forward Goncalo Guedes and another strike from Bruno Fernandes secured a comfortable success. It was a welcome boost for the European Champions, who hadn't won since March. They were held in draws against Tunisia (2-2) and Belgium (0-0) in their previous two friendlies. Portugal meets Spain in their World Cup opener on the 15th of June.

Uruguay Will Head to Russia on A Winning Note

Uruguay will head to Russia on a winning note after beating Uzbekistan in a friendly in a chilly warm-up. The win was a third in a row for the South Americans, and they have lost just once in their last nine games. Uruguay got the breakthrough after 31 minutes when Giorgian De Arrascaeta fired home from fifteen metres following good work from Edinson Cavani and Luis Suarez. Suarez doubled their lead eight minutes into the second half when he slotted home a penalty, and Jose Maria Gimenez headed home a corner in 72 min to make it 3-0. Uzbekistan was then reduced to ten men when Komilov Akromjom was sent off.

4 DAYS TO GO

Salah's Availability Uncertain

Star forward Mohamed Salah is still no certainty to face Uruguay in Egypt's World Cup opener against Uruguay. Egypt star Mohamed Salah's availability for their World Cup opener against Uruguay is "uncertain" despite joining his team's training session Saturday. Salah, 25, is still recovering from a shoulder injury suffered in Liverpool's Champions League final loss to Real Madrid last month. The superstar forward—who scored 44 goals for his club in 2017-18—joined his international teammates in training but was largely restricted to being a spectator. Egypt team doctor Mohamed Abou El-Ela said there were still no guarantees Salah would play a part against Uruguay in their Group A opener Friday. "Everything looks good. His condition is comfortable, but playing against Uruguay is uncertain," he said. "We'll take our decision after two days as everything will be clear. Our goal is to keep him safe, and he will play if he's 100 per cent fit." After facing Uruguay, Egypt meets Russia (the 19th of June) and Saudi Arabia (the 25th of June).

Argentina Must Rise to Messi's Standards

Javier Mascherano said that Lionel Messi will set Argentina's standards at the World Cup in Russia. Javier Mascherano hopes Lionel Messi will be "the best version of himself" at the World Cup while acknowledging that the Barcelona star sets a standard the rest of the squad must strive to match. Messi will arrive at his fourth World Cup hoping to go one better than the runners-up medal he won in 2014 by inspiring Argentina to glory. His former Camp Nou colleague Mascherano made no secret of the importance of the five-time Ballon d'Or winner showing his best form. Mascherano, who has 143 caps for Argentina and won five LA Liga titles alongside Messi at Barcelona before joining Hebei China Fortune, also underlined the strength of Jorge Sampaoli's defence. "One wishes for this coming World Cup that Leo can be the best version of himself because the aspirations of the whole squad depend on this version," Mascherano told The Guardian. "It's clear Leo conditions our collective performance; I hope, as his teammates, we can meet his standards." For years, the talk has been of Argentina's strong point being the offensive side, the attack, and clearly, we do have players with immense talent up front. But I think what has made these recent teams so competitive has been the ability to find a defensive equilibrium."

Reflecting on Argentina's journey to the 2014 final under Alejandro Sabella, the 34-year-old pointed to the importance of a clear vision going into the tournament in Russia. Argentina faces Iceland in their Group D opener on the 16th of June with the memory of defeat to Germany in the final four years ago still fresh in their minds. "It was a unique experience because we had never lived or experienced anything like what happened in 2014—it was spectacular," said Mascherano. "The World Cup itself sets the pace and indicates what we can and can't do: we changed the way we played, the system, as we went along, but always with total clarity about what we were doing. That was what led us to the final." The conviction of our idea of doing things in a certain way, up to the very last minute. And if you look back, I think it was

Argentina's best match in years."

Pogba Is Most Probably in The Starting XI

Didier Deschamps is keeping the faith with under-fire midfielder Paul Pogba. Paul Pogba is almost certain to start France's World Cup opener against Australia. At the same time, Olivier Giroud will also be available, Didier Deschamps has confirmed. A debate has raged over whether Pogba merits a place in midfield, with the Manchester United man failing to convince in recent matches. He was jeered by his own fans during the 3-1 friendly win over Italy and failed to inspire France in an underwhelming 1-1 draw against the youthful United States on Saturday. Deschamps, however, is continuing to back the 25-year-old, telling broadcaster Telefoot it is "very likely" he will be in the starting XI in Kazan on the 16th of June. The boss of Les Bleus also offered assurances over the fitness of Giroud, who was bloodied and forced off following a head clash with USA defender Matt Miazga. "Olivier Giroud has a beautiful cut of 6 centimetres. But he will be able to face Australia," Deschamps said. France's other Group C opponents are Denmark and Peru.

Messi Considers Retirement

Lionel Messi is unsure if he will continue playing for Argentina beyond the World Cup. The 30-year-old briefly stepped away from the Albiceleste in 2016 and is considering bringing a permanent close to an international career that began in 2005. His long stint in the national team has been marked with near misses, including a defeat to Germany in the 2014 World Cup decider and back-to-back final failures at the Copa America. Messi, who was named player of the tournament four years ago, believes his country's media have undervalued Argentina's accomplishments and says the trip to Russia could be his last. "I don't know. It will depend on how we do, how it ends," the star attacker told Sport.

"The fact we've lost three finals now has led to some complicated moments with the Argentine press due to the differences in seeing what it means to reach a final. It is not easy, and [reaching three finals] has to be appreciated. It's true that winning them is important, but getting there is not easy." Should they reach the knockout stages, Messi expects Argentina's bid for a third World Cup title to face stiff opposition from Brazil, Germany, Spain, France, and Belgium. However, he insists Jorge Sampaoli's side have nothing to fear in Russia. "There are a lot of very good players, but we also have quality players that any national team would want. We don't envy anyone," the skipper added. Argentina commences their campaign against Iceland in Moscow on the 16th of June before further Group D clashes with Croatia.

3 DAYS TO GO

Neymar returns

Brazil scored three superbly taken goals to beat feisty Austria 3-0 in sweltering conditions on Sunday and put the finishing touches to their impressive World Cup preparation. Gabriel Jesus, Neymar, and Philippe Coutinho shared the goals for the five-time champions, who showed great patience in the first half as they worked on breaking Austria down before turning on the style after the interval. Neymar started a game for the first time since injuring his metatarsal in February. However, he played in the second half of the game against Croatia when he celebrated his return with a goal. It was also the first the quartet of Neymar, Jesus, Coutinho, and Willian had started a game together. Neymar, substituted in the 83rd min, was on the receiving end of some tough challenges and needed treatment after a tackle from behind from Aleksander Dragovic, who was booked. With the temperature hot enough for water breaks, tempers frayed as Casemiro replied with a rough tackle of his own. Marko Arnautovic gave Brazil a couple of early frights before the South Americans went ahead in the 36th min, Jesus' scoring with a delightful, dinked effort from a difficult angle after Marcelo's shot rebounded to him; it was his 10th goal in 17th internationals. Neymar's goal in the 83rd min was even better as he collected the ball on the left of the area, performed a drag-back which left Aleksander Dragovic on the ground and sent his shot between goalkeeper Heinz Linder's legs. Neymar's goal holds him level with Romario's total of international goals, making him Brazil's third joint-top scorer after Pele (77) and Ronaldo (62).

Spain Laboured to A Narrow Victory Against Tunisia

Spain laboured to a narrow 1-0 victory over Tunisia in an underwhelming World Cup in Krasnodar. The 2010 champions remain unbeaten under coach Julen Lopetegui, who took over 20 matches ago after the Roja's elimination from Euro 2016 in the last 16 at the hands of Italy. Iago Aspas scored the only goal against fellow World Cup qualifiers Tunisia seven minutes from the end. But Lopetegui's search for a consistent centre-forward was no clearer despite a solid showing from Brazil-born Diego Costa. The Atletico Madrid forward set up Aspa's winner and was a nuisance throughout for the African defenders.

Spain dominated the ball but gave Tunisia some good scoring chances. Spain began their Group B campaign against the European champions Portugal on the 15th of June, while Tunisia faced England in Group G 3 days later.

Paul Pogba put in an improved performance, but France looked flat in a 1-1 World Cup warm-up draw against the United States in Lyon.

Julian Green gave the US, who failed to make it to Russia, the lead on the stroke of half-time, but teenage starlet Kylian Mbappe equalised for the hosts. Pogba had been jeered a week ago in a 3-1 victory over Italy. Still, it was his past that teed up Mbappe to save face for the Euro 2016 finalists in a match they were expected to win. With perhaps one eye on their opening World Cup clash against Australia, 2-1 winners over Hungary earlier in the day, on the 16th of June, France was pedestrian for long periods. "We lacked a bit of juice, but we created enough chances to win," said coach Didier Deschamps on TF1. "But that's the way it goes, against a young United States team that was very generous, who didn't leave us a lot of space and try to defend very well."

2 DAYS TO GO

Giroud Should Be Fit to Play for France

Oliver Giroud should be fit to play France's World Cup opening game against Australia after leading the fridge with a bloodied forehead in the 1-1 draw against the United States, coach Didier Deschamps said. Deschamps added that midfielder Paul Pogba was also very likely to start Les Bleu's first game in Group C. Giroud has a beautiful card of 6 cm, but he should be ready," Deschamps said.

Iceland Comical Debut

Iceland needed police help to keep their World Cup plans on track after coach Heimer Hallgrimsson put his bag on the wrong bus in a comical start to their debut campaign. Hallgrimsson's bag was on a bus headed for Northern Iceland rather than the team coach bound for the airport. This slip delayed the group's departure by half an hour while the item was recovered. "It was good for the guys that they can laugh at me," said Hallgrimsson after the team's first World Cup training session close to the city of Gelendzhik on Russia's sunny Black Sea coast. "Hopefully, it's the only mistake of the tournament."

A-Z Guide to the World Cup

Iceland coach Heimer Hallgrimsson used to be a dentist. And he keeps his hand in. “It’s good you take time off football for some time and do something different. Some coaches play golf. I do dentistry.” What teams will be going for the trophy has 4.9 KG of gold in it. Weight is a little over 6 KG. A ticket or a visa isn’t enough to get into Russia, and the stadium is for the matches. You need a Fan ID—send in your passport data, address, and phone number, which is processed by the SFB, the successor agency to the Soviet KGB. The final ID doubles as a Russian Visa and transport pass from June four to the 25th of July.

When you play to win, you got to look the part. And if there is such a category, the best dressed will go to Nigeria. The team’s lime green zigzag shirts had a staggering 3M pre-order online, queues stretched two blocks, and the kits sold out in 20 minutes. Egypt will have the oldest player, goalkeeper Essam El Hadary, aged 45 years and four months. Incredibly, this will be his first World Cup.

The heavyweight title goes to Panama’s Roman Torres, weighing 99 KG.

Iceland is the smallest country to qualify in the history of the competition. And then there’s Italy, four times the World Cup winner didn’t qualify. One and a half of football’s greatest rivalry. What Lionel Messi and Cristiano Ronaldo did this month established either of the greatest of all time. The World Cup’s next destination is Qatar. The tournament may even be a 42-man tournament.

The Sport's Beating Heart

The eyes of the world will turn to Russia this week for the World Cup, but it is far away. You must look to find the Sport's beating heart, war-ravaged streets, and poverty-stricken slams, whether the simple act of scoring a goal transcends the grind of everyday life. For every girl celebrated by the 32 teams at the phone gathering of football superstars, thousands more will be scored on makeshift in Yemen, Somalia, Gaza, and beyond. They will not be recorded for posterity and reply to thousands of times over. But they will not be forgotten, and the score is, for a few minutes, at least, can dream of being a hero. "My favourite player is Argentina's Lionel Messi. When I score a goal, I feel happy and successful; I am pleased that my teammates are also happy with me," 14-year-old Mohammad Ali Kargbo said after scoring a goal in Freetown, Sierra Leone.

In the four years since FIFA's extravaganza, most played out across Brazil's football governing body has been dragged by corruption scandals and provoking accusations from fans that the beautiful game has been poisoned by greed. The month-long do not mind in Russia is officially costing an eye-watering 683 billion roubles ($11 billion). Many of the players are millionaires many times over. Dreams cost nothing, though. Try telling 12-year-old Aoud Mustafa, who plays with his friends in Syria's Zaizon refugee camp in Deraa, that soccer has lost its soul. "When ice cold, I feel very happy, and I also feel stronger and faster than my friends," he said after a game on a dusty patch of earth.

The World Cup will be played in 12 ultra-modern stadiums across Russia, most newly built, which sums of money would lead to lead a life-changing for millions of vulnerable people across Africa and the middle east yet access to a ball and a goal, be it a couple of chunks of masonry, two twisted sticks in the desert or the remains of a bombed-out building can provide a theatre of dreams rescued from the horrors of armed conflict for the daily struggle of a life lived in the most challenging circumstances. For one young boy playing in the playground of a bomb-damaged School in Benghazi, Libya, the simple act of scoring a goal represents a homecoming of sorts, the chance of a return to a semblance of normality. "I feel joyful because I'm playing my own area, which I have been unable to do for more than three years because of the word," he said.

Indian Fans Are Serious

The FIFA World Cup is two days away, and even though the Indian team is not a part of it, Indian football fans are eagerly awaiting the best single sports tournament in the world. According to figures provided by broadcasters, more than a hundred million Indians watched the 2014 World Cup on TV, and the number is expected to only go higher this time. In the absence of a home team to support, most Indian football wildly adopted their second home team. Gurgaon-based software engineer and Spain supporter Deepak Yadav says inverted, we, Indians, are lucky that we get to choose your favourite teams, and we do that over time, carefully. It would be great to have India play in the World Cup and behind them, but till that happens, we all have our own teams until that happens. “The absence does not indicate that Indians just casually support their favourite teams. The fans are devoted to the Sport.

Salah Might Win the Ballon d’Or.

Ronaldo has shared the Ballon d’Or with Lionel Messi since 2008. Still, Cristiano Ronaldo believes the two-man race could soon be cracked open. Cristiano Ronaldo believes Liverpool sensation Mohamed Salah is a genuine contender to break his and Lionel Messi’s decade-long dominance of the Ballon d’Or. Salah enjoyed a stunning debut season, scooping the Premier League Golden Boot en route to netting 44 goals in all competitions. His sparkling form underpinned the Reds’ surge to a surprise Champions League final appearance against Ronaldo’s Real Madrid. However, the fairy-tale ended in tears as a shoulder injury forced him out in the early stages of Kyiv’s 3-1 defeat. Ronaldo, who has shared five Ballon d’Or apiece with Messi since 2008, hopes the Egypt international will be fit to prove his class at the World Cup.

“Salah has been one of the revelations of the year,” Ronaldo told reporters.

“I hope his injury in the final in Kyiv doesn’t keep him out.

“Many people talk about the battle for the Ballon d’Or between Cristiano Ronaldo and Lionel Messi, but there are other players who have a chance to enter the race. Salah is certainly one of them.”

Ronaldo Has Set His Sights on The World Cup

With a fifth Champions League crown secured, Ronaldo has set his sights on leading Portugal to more silverware in what will be his fourth World Cup.

The 33-year-old admits a tough Group B opener against Spain on the 15th of June is not ideal. Still, he remains confident the European champions will reach the knockout rounds.

"A defeat on the first day puts you in a bad way for the rest of the tournament, so it's important to start well," he said. "But I believe both Spain and Portugal will reach the next round. To win the World Cup would be a dream for Portugal, but to do it, we have to play the same way we did in Euro 2016, as a team and all together."

1 DAY TO GO

Belgium Desperate to Win the Trophy

De Bruyne said Roberto Martinez's men were full of belief, with their first outing a clash against Panama Monday. "We know this Belgium squad is special, and, of course, we're desperate to win a trophy," he said. "We have the belief, but there can only be one nation that wins the World Cup—but we're ready for the fight."

The 2026 World Cup May Take Place in North America

FIFA members will decide whether the 2026 World Cup will be played in North America or Morocco, taking football's greatest showpiece to Africa for just the second time. The choice is clear—between a slick bid based on gleaming stadiums in the US, Mexico, or Canada or an ambitious attempt from Morocco based on largely unbuilt facilities. On the eve of the 2018 FIFA World Cup in Russia, 207 FIFA member nations will cast their vote in a congress of world football's governing body. Morocco's bid for 2026 was only cleared to advance to the runoff vote this month, despite an evaluation report which classified the North African nation's stadiums, accommodation, and transport as high-risk. Morocco received only 2.7 out of 5, with red flags raised over several critical bid components. A FIFA summary of the task force's findings warned, "The amount of new infrastructure required for the Morocco 2026 bid to become a reality cannot be overstated." The report left the US-Canada-Mexico bid as the clear front-runner after giving it a rating of 4 out of 5. But the North American bid has been dogged by concerns that the vote could become a referendum on the popularity of US president Donald Trump.

Neymar Lost the Fear to Play

According to goalkeeper Alisson, Brazil star Neymar is growing in confidence and has "lost the fear to play" ahead of the World Cup. Neymar has starred on his return from a foot injury, scoring in Brazil's friendly wins over Croatia and Austria earlier this month. The 26-year-old was sidelined for three months after needing surgery, but his return has been a boost to Tite's men before Russia 2018. Alisson praised his teammate for the way he has returned as Brazil prepares for Group E matches against Switzerland, Costa Rica, and Serbia. "Neymar is doing very well, fortunately. I believe they dealt well with his recovery process. He had a full clinical recovery," he told a news conference Tuesday. "Of course, in the beginning, when he started working with the ball and working with the team, we were extra careful. He had to deal with fear, which is normal after such a severe injury. And we also tried to take good care of him in the training sessions." Gradually, he became more confident. He started in the second half of the first game [against Croatia], he helped us, and he lost the fear of playing. And in the last game, he played well, and I think that made him more confident. We need Neymar on the field." Brazil begins their World Cup campaign with a clash against Switzerland.

Groups:

Group Matches:

14 June	Match 1	Russia vs Saudi Arabia	20:30	Luzhniki Stadium, [illegible]
15 June	Match 2	Egypt vs Uruguay	17:30	Ekaterinburg Arena, Ekaterinburg
15 June	Match 3	Morocco vs Iran	20:30	Saint Petersburg Stadium, Saint Petersburg
15 June	Match 4	Portugal vs Spain	23:30	Fisht Stadium, Sochi
16 June	Match 5	France vs Australia	15:30	Kazan Arena, Kazan
[illegible]	Match 6	Argentina vs Iceland	18:30	Spartak Stadium, Moscow
[illegible]	Match 7	Peru vs Denmark	21:30	Mordovia Arena, Saransk
[illegible]	Match 8	Croatia vs Nigeria	00:30	Kaliningrad Stadium, Kaliningrad
17 June	Match 9	Costa Rica vs Serbia	17:30	Samara Arena, Samara
17 June	Match 10	Germany vs Mexico	20:30	Luzhniki Stadium, Moscow
17 June	Match 11	Brazil vs Switzerland	23:30	Rostov Arena, Rostov-On-Don
18 June	Match 12	Sweden vs South Korea	17:30	Nizhny Novgorod Stadium
18 June	Match 13	Belgium vs Panama	20:30	Fisht Stadium, Sochi
18 June	Match 14	Tunisia vs England	23:30	Volgograd Arena, Volgograd
19 June	Match 15	Colombia vs Japan	17:30	Mordovia Arena, Saransk
19 June	Match 16	Poland vs Senegal	20:30	Spartak Stadium, Moscow
19 June	Match 17	Russia vs Egypt	23:30	Saint Petersburg Stadium, Saint Petersburg
20 June	Match 18	Portugal vs Morocco	17:30	Luzhniki Stadium, Moscow
20 June	Match 19	Uruguay vs Saudi Arabia	20:30	Rostov Arena, Rostov-On-Don
20 June	Match 20	Iran vs Spain	23:30	Kazan Arena, Kazan
21 June	Match 21	Denmark vs Australia	17:30	Samara Arena, Samara
21 June	Match 22	France vs Peru	20:30	Ekaterinburg Arena, Ekaterinburg
21 June	Match 23	Argentina vs Croatia	23:30	Nizhny Novgorod Stadium
22 June	Match 24	Brazil vs Costa Rica	17:30	Saint Petersburg Stadium, Saint Petersburg
22 June	Match 25	Nigeria vs Iceland	20:30	Volgograd Arena, Volgograd
22 June	Match 26	Serbia vs Switzerland	23:30	Kaliningrad Stadium, Kaliningrad
[illegible]	[illegible]	[illegible] vs Tunisia	[illegible]	Spartak Stadium, Moscow
23 June	Match 28	South Korea vs Mexico	20:30	Rostov Arena, Rostov-on-Don
23 June	Match 29	Germany vs Sweden	23:30	Fisht Stadium, Sochi
24 June	Match 30	England vs Panama	17:30	Nizhny Novgorod Stadium
24 June	Match 31	Japan vs Senegal	20:30	Ekaterinburg Arena, Ekaterinburg
24 June	Match 32	Poland vs Colombia	23:30	Kazan Arena, Kazan
25 June	Match 33	Uruguay vs Russia	19:30	Samara Arena, Samara
25 June	Match 34	Saudi Arabia vs Egypt	19:30	Volgograd Arena, Volgograd
25 June	Match 35	Spain vs Morocco	23:30	Kaliningrad Stadium, Kaliningrad
25 June	Match 36	Iran vs Portugal	23:30	Mordovia Arena, Saransk
26 June	Match 37	Australia vs Peru	19:30	Fisht Stadium, Sochi
26 June	Match 38	Denmark vs France	19:30	Luzhniki Stadium, Moscow
26 June	Match 39	Nigeria vs Argentina	23:30	Saint Petersburg Stadium, Saint Petersburg
26 June	Match 40	Iceland vs Croatia	23:30	Rostov Arena, Rostov-on-Don
27 June	Match 41	South Korea vs Germany	19:30	Kazan Arena, Kazan
27 June	Match 42	Mexico vs Sweden	19:30	Ekaterinburg Arena, Ekaterinburg
27 June	Match 43	Serbia vs Brazil	23:30	Spartak Stadium, Moscow
27 June	Match 44	Switzerland vs Costa Rica	23:30	Nizhny Novgorod Stadium
28 June	Match 45	Japan vs Poland	19:30	Volgograd Arena, Volgograd
28 June	Match 46	Senegal vs Colombia	19:30	Samara Arena, Samara
28 June	Match 47	Panama vs Tunisia	23:30	Mordovia Arena, Saransk
28 June	Match 48	England vs Belgium	23:30	Kaliningrad Stadium Kaliningrad

Knockouts:

30 June	Match 49	Winner Group C vs Runner-up Group D	19:30	Kazan Arena, Kazan
30 June	Match 50	Winner Group A vs Runner-up Group B	23:30	Fisht Stadium, Sochi
1 July	Match 51	Winner Group B vs Runner-up Group A	19:30	Luzhniki Stadium, Moscow
1 July	Match 52	Winner Group D vs Runner-up Group C	23:30	Nizhny Novgorod Stadium
2 July	Match 53	Winner Group E vs Runner-up Group F	19:30	Samara Arena, Samara
2 July	Match 54	Winner Group G vs Runner-up Group H	23:30	Rostov Arena, Rostov-on-Don
3 July	Match 55	Winner Group F vs Runner-up Group E	19:30	Saint Petersburg Stadium St. Petersburg
3 July	Match 56	Winner Group H vs Runner-up Group G	23:30	Spartak Stadium, Moscow
QUARTERFINALS				
6 July	Match 57	Winner Match 49 vs Winner Match 50	19:30	Nizhny Novgorod Stadium
6 July	Match 58	Winner Match 53 vs Winner Match 54	23:30	Kazan Arena, Kazan
7 July	Match 59	Winner Match 55 vs Winner Match 56	19:30	Samara Arena, Samara
7 July	Match 60	Winner Match 51 vs Winner Match 52	23:30	Fisht Stadium, Sochi
SEMIFINALS				
10 July	Match 61	Winner Match 57 vs Winner Match 58	23:30	Saint Petersburg Stadium St. Petersburg
11 July	Match 62	Winner Match 59 vs Winner Match 60	23:30	Luzhniki Stadium, Moscow
THIRD PLACE PLAY-OFF				
14 July	Match 63	Loser Match 61 vs Loser Match 62	19:30	Saint Petersburg Stadium St. Petersburg
FINAL				
15 July	**Match 64**	**Winner Match 61 vs Winner Match 62**	**20:30**	**Luzhniki Stadium, Moscow**

WORLD CUP OPENING DAY

History of Soccer Balls:

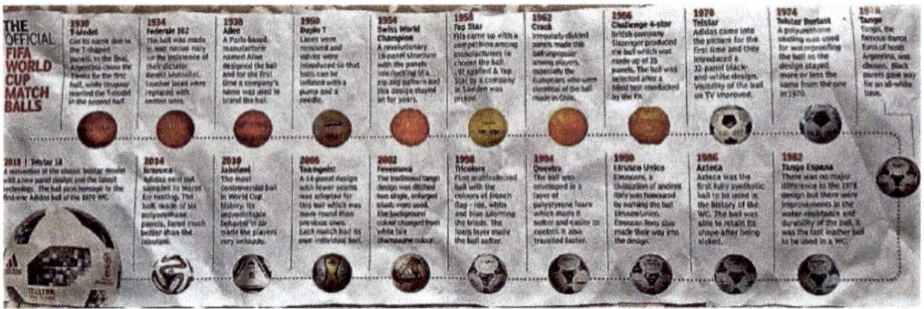

Lopetegui Put in Place Hierro in Charge

After soaring without hitting an Air pocket since the 21st of July 2016, Spain hurtled a crisis on the eve of the World Cup start. Julen Lopetegui, who replaced Vincent Del Bosque as coach, was sacked on Wednesday at Krasnodar, Spain's training base for Russia 2018. Lopetegui had a fine record, remaining unbeaten in 14 out of 20 games, even fashioning Spain as one of Russia's favourites but failed to complete even two years in office. Fernando Hierro, the team's sporting director, has been appointed Spain's head coach and will lead their campaign in Russia. A former Real Madrid mainstay, Hierro's last coaching job was with Spanish second-division side Real Oviedo, to an eighth-place finish. Real Madrid's hasty announcement of Lopetegui as Zidane's successor stirred a hornet's nest.

The Spanish base at Krasnodar, On the Kuban, turned into a beehive of negotiations and counterintelligence activity, demoting the small matter of a World Cup game against Portugal in two days to the lowest on the priority checklist. Moments after Real's announcement, Spanish Football Federation President Luis Rubiales flew out of Moscow late Tuesday night, leaving the FIFA Congress to take charge of the situation. A twice-delayed press conference followed, and the declaration that Spain most dreaded was made "We have been forced to dispense with the national coach. We wish him the best of luck. We will have to carry on with the work he has developed," Rubiales said. "The problem is how things have been done with the total absence of participation of the Spanish Football Federation; that is something we cannot ignore. Lopetegui is an impeccable professional, but the process is important," the President said.

Rubiales could not have dreamt of such a situation developing a month into office. "Five minutes before issuing the press release, the club informed us. The federation cannot remain on the sidelines during the negotiation with one of its workers and find out five minutes before the issuance of a statement. We are being forced to act. I know there's going to be criticism whatever I do. Still, the values of the federation must be defended," he added, "I do not feel betrayed. While Lopetegui was with us, he has done an impeccable job." Reports from Krasnodar say that captain Sergio Ramos argued hard for Lopetegui to stay in charge for the duration of the World Cup. The sacking became the talk of the World Cup. The German team, training on the outskirts of Moscow, was also avidly discussing a surprise development." Coach Joachim Loew said, "Lopetegui's dismissal was a huge surprise for me. I do not know the reason, but such a situation the day before the World Cup starts is serious because it can destabilise the Spanish team. I hope that the dismissal will not affect the preparation of the team for the World Cup matches." Loew wished Hierro good luck.

Cahill Ready to Dance on the Biggest Stage

Tim Cahill could join a select group if he finds the net for Australia at the 2018 World Cup in Russia. Evergreen Australia striker Tim Cahill is ready for "the big dance" as he attempts to waltz into World Cup folklore. Cahill could join Brazil legend Pele and former Germany strikers Miroslav Klose and Uwe Seeler as the only players to have scored at four World Cups should he get on the scoresheet in Russia. The 38-year-old is more of a squad player nowadays after previously being the fulcrum of a Socceroo's side that continues to grow on the global stage. But he has shelved all talk of international retirement until after the tournament. Speaking ahead of Australia's Group C opener against France on Saturday, he told a news conference: "It's not a dress rehearsal; the big dance is here. This is where you must step up. The fact is we train today, we train the day after, and we play France. That's all that's in my mind." As for joining Pele, Klose, and Seeler, he added: "I have put in so much effort to be here. To get on the pitch would be one step; to score would just be amazing. To join the list of names that are on there now would be priceless." You have to take your moments. If I get on the pitch, I know I am going to try to make something happen. I would love to join the greats, being an Australian, being someone who has broken all barriers." While Cahill is at one end of his career, the France side that will take the field in Kazan will feature some of the game's greatest young talents, led by Kylian Mbappe and Ousmane Dembele.

The development of Les Bleus under Didier Deschamps has been gradual—defeat on home soil to Portugal in the European Championship final two years ago remains an open wound—and their time may not come here in Russia, but rather in Qatar in 2022. But French Football Federation President Noel Le Graet is encouraged by the emergence of a new, zestful side that appears to be shorn of the cliques that have ravaged previous generations. Le Graet said: "When you look at the number of young players we have, we can consider this to be a good France team." And when you see Mbappe answering the media's questions with an implausible maturity, it's extraordinary. "When the players are with the national team, they behave in an exemplary way. The change is clear. Deschamps has put a lot of effort into making the conditions ideal."

Mbappe sustained a knock in training on Tuesday but declared himself "100 per cent fit" 24 hours later and is likely to lead the line.

This Could Be Neymar's Time

Hopes are high for Brazil ahead of the World Cup in Russia, where Neymar will look to lead his side to glory. Former Argentina international Javier Zanetti believes Neymar is nearing the same level as serial Ballon d'Or winners Lionel Messi and Cristiano Ronaldo. The Brazil international was the star of the show for his nation in their home World Cup four years ago, only for his involvement to be cut short following an injury suffered in the quarterfinal victory over Colombia. Neymar subsequently missed the semi-final against Germany, where his team suffered a humbling 7-1 defeat against eventual winners Germany but will hope to lead his side to glory this year. Already capped 85 times, Neymar caught the headlines last year with a record transfer from Barcelona to Paris Saint-Germain as he continued his quest to become the world's best. While Messi and Ronaldo are still viewed as the top two, Zanetti feels the PSG forward - who has recovered from a foot injury in time to feature in Russia is not far behind. "Neymar is very strong, has great quality, and is very close to Messi and Ronaldo," he told Media Set. "I believe that this World Cup can be that of his consecration." Brazil begins their campaign against Switzerland on Sunday before completing their Group E fixtures against Costa Rica and Serbia.

The Opening Ceremony

The loudest cheer was not reserved for Robbie Williams, anyway.

Regaling The packed crowd at the Luzhniki stadium in Moscow, Robbie Williams and the famous Russian opera singer Aida Garifullina give a rousing performance in the opening ceremony of the FIFA Russia World Cup. It was President Vladimir Putin for whom the Russians cheered their heart out. Not once but twice, and the President stopped to take a breath. Dapperly dressed in a suit, the Russian President spoke for about two minutes, and the crowd lapped it up. He said hosting the World Cup is like love at first sight and welcomed all to come and enjoy Russia. He recalled Russia's first international game in 1897 and sized on football's power to unite, defying differences in language, ideology, and faith. Williams belted out, "Let me entertain you. In what is, I would love to party like a Russian."

RUSSIA VS SAUDI ARABIA

STADIUM - LUZHNIKI

MATCH STATS

RUSSIA		SAUDI ARABIA
14	Total Attempts	6
7	Attempts on Target	0
6	Corners	2
343	Total Passes	558
15	Total Crosses	6
58	Balls Recovered	52
80	Duels Won	66
22	Fouls Committed	10

RUSSIA 5
Gazinsky 12; Cheryshev 43' 90+1', Dzyuba 71', Golovin 90+4'

SAUDI ARABIA 0

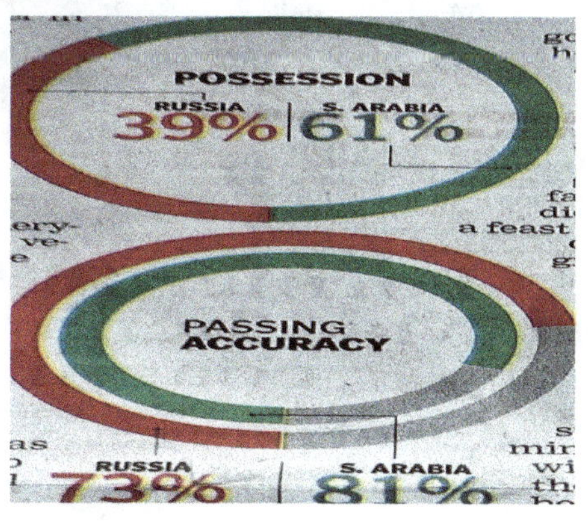

EGYPT VS URUGUAY

STADIUM - EKATERINBURG

MATCH STATS

EGYPT		URUGUAY
8	Total Shots	15
3	Shots on Target	4
0	Corners	5
427	Total Passes	586
11	Total Crosses	22
70	Balls Recovered	76
45	Duels Won	67
12	Fouls Committed	6

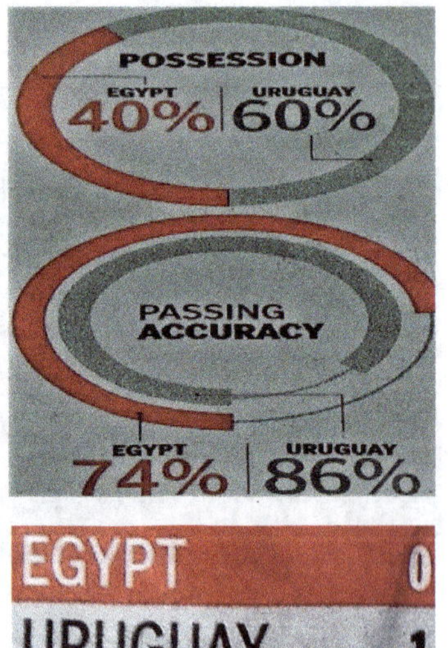

MOROCCO VS IRAN

STADIUM - S.T. PETERSBURG

MOROCCO 0

IRAN 1

Bouhaddouz 90+5-og

MATCH STATS

MOROCCO		IRAN
13	Total Shots	9
3	Shots on Target	2
5	Corners	2
462	Total Passes	217
15	Total Crosses	8
57	Balls Recovered	44
58	Duels Won	63
22	Fouls Committed	14
68%	Possession	32%
81%	Passing Accuracy	58%

Nigerian Fans Chicken Requests Stump Hosts

Nigerian fans cheering on their national team in Saturday's match against Croatia will be missing an important item in their supporter's tool kit: chickens. Live chickens are sometimes seen in matches in Nigeria, where fans paint them in the green and white colours of the national flag before holding them aloft and leading the crowd to chant. But officials in the Russian exclave of Kaliningrad, Where Nigeria takes on Croatia, have said animals will not be allowed in the stadium. Andrei Yermak, Minister for Culture and Tourism, said some Nigerian fans had asked if bringing chickens to the match would be possible.

ARGENTINA VS ICELAND

STADIUM – S.P.A.R.T.A.K.

MATCH STATS

ARGENTINA		ICELAND
27	Total Shots	8
7	Shots on Target	2
10	Corners	2
751	Total Passes	208
25	Total Crosses	10
50	Balls Recovered	44
66	Duels Won	56
10	Fouls Committed	15

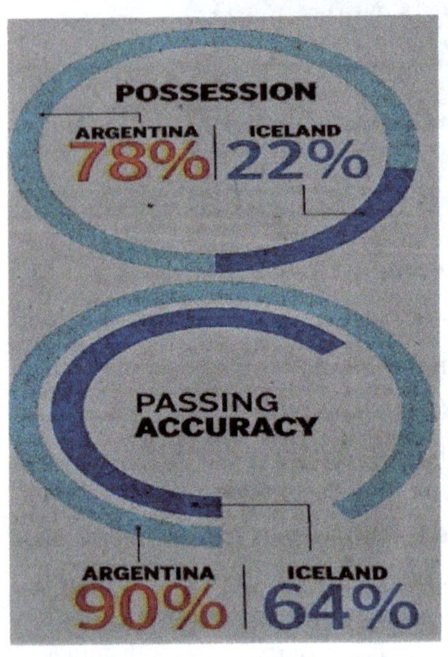

FRANCE VS AUSTRALIA

STADIUM - KAZAN ARENA

FRANCE 2

Griezmann 58-pen, Pogba 81

AUSTRALIA 1

Jedinak 62-pen

MATCH STATS

FRANCE		AUSTRALIA
13	Total Shots	6
6	Shots on Target	1
5	Corners	1
508	Total Passes	406
15	Total Crosses	9
60	Balls Recovered	58
53	Duels Won	55
16	Fouls Committed	19
55%	Possession	45%
84%	Passing Accuracy	80%

PERU VS DENMARK

STADIUM - MORDOVIA ARENA

Who's The Goat, Ronaldo or Messi

G. O. A. T, says the urban dictionary, stands for greatest of all time. And on Friday night, after firing home an irrefutable penalty, Portugal's talisman Cristiano Ronaldo made it clear who is thinks is the GOAT of world football. The 33-year-old striker scratched and imagined a goatee, cocking a snook at a cheeky ad that shows Argentina's wizard Lionel Messi with a goat. On Saturday evening, as Messi faltered with the spot kick against Iceland, his great rival might have enjoyed a chuckle or two. Ronaldo was on stoppable the night before. His 88-minute freekick soared above the wall and dipped in as if on command. Portugal's one-man Army had scored a superb World Cup hat-trick and single-handedly secured a 3-3 draw against the mighty SPAIN.

GERMANY VS MEXICO

STADIUM – LUZHNIKI

MATCH STATS

GERMANY		MEXICO
26	Total Shots	15
9	Shots on Target	4
8	Corners	1
597	Total Passes	302
27	Total Crosses	7
54	Balls Recovered	54
46	Duels Won	58
10	Fouls Committed	16

POSSESSION

GERMANY 67% | MEXICO 33%

PASSING ACCURACY

GERMANY 86% | MEXICO 76%

COSTA RICA VS SERBIA

STADIUM – SAMARA

COSTA RICA 0

SERBIA 1

Kolarov 56

MATCH STATS

C. RICA		SERBIA
10	Total Shots	10
3	Shots on Target	3
5	Corners	4
450	Total Passes	415
22	Total Crosses	14
62	Balls Recovered	59
68	Duels Won	79
18	Fouls Committed	15
53%	Possession	47%
80%	Passing Accuracy	78%

CROATIA VS NIGERIA

STADIUM - KALININGRAD

MATCH STATS

CROATIA		NIGERIA
12	Total Shots	14
2	Shots on Target	2
6	Corners	5
481	Total Passes	395
21	Total Crosses	17
66	Balls Recovered	55
64	Duels Won	72
20	Fouls Committed	16
55%	Possession	45%
80%	Passing Accuracy	79%

Rakitic—A Bit Too Carried Away

Croatian midfielder Ivan Rakitic was perhaps a bit too carried away celebrating after their win over Nigeria. The Barcelona star left the pitch with only his socks and underwear, having given away his jersey shorts and boots to fans.

Faulty Positioning

The Argentina squad worked perfectly lined up for the national anthem ahead of their game against Iceland—all except Willy Caballero. The Chelsea keeper stood with his back to Messi, probably looking towards the national flag.

SWEDEN VS SOUTH KOREA

STADIUM - NIZHNY NOVGOROD STADIUM

MATCH STATS

15	Total Shots	5
4	Shots on Target	0
6	Corners	5
446	Total Passes	359
20	Total Crosses	13
41	Balls Recovered	52
71	Duels Won	62
20	Fouls Committed	23
56%	Possession	44%
81%	Passing Accuracy	78%

SWEDEN 1

Granqvist 65-pen

SOUTH KOREA

BELGIUM VS PANAMA

STADIUM - FISHT STADIUM

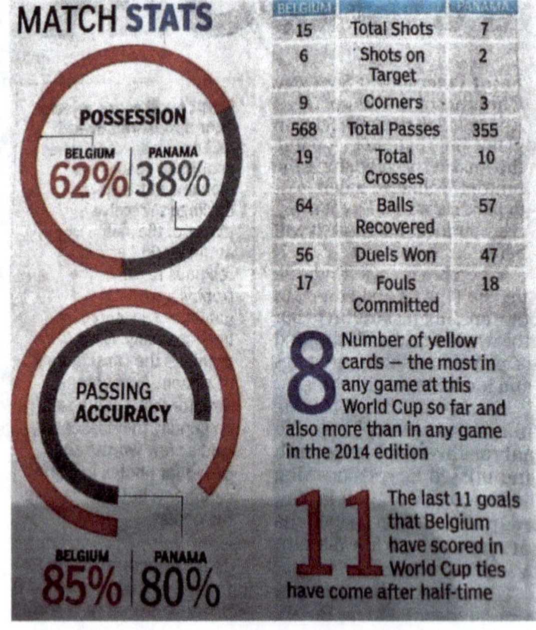

MATCH STATS

POSSESSION

BELGIUM 62% | PANAMA 38%

PASSING ACCURACY

BELGIUM 85% | PANAMA 80%

Belgium		Panama
15	Total Shots	7
6	Shots on Target	2
9	Corners	3
568	Total Passes	355
19	Total Crosses	10
64	Balls Recovered	57
56	Duels Won	47
17	Fouls Committed	18

8 Number of yellow cards – the most in any game at this World Cup so far and also more than in any game in the 2014 edition

11 The last 11 goals that Belgium have scored in World Cup ties have come after half-time

Nobody Comes to the World Cup to Make the Numbers

This is the first World Cup where Brazil, Argentina, Germany, and Portugal failed to win their opening matches.

Five of the top six in the FIFA rankings have played in Russia, and none has won. Only two of the top dozen teams have victories.

Top-ranked Germany lost to number 15, Mexico.

Second-ranked Brazil tied for number six with Switzerland.

Number four, Portugal drew 10th-ranked Spain.

Number five, Argentina tied 22nd ranked Iceland.

Among other teams in the top 12, only number seven France (Over number 36 Australia) and co-No. 12 Denmark (against number 11 Peru) have victories.

At the time of writing, number three Belgium, number eight Poland, and co-No. 12 England haven't played, and number nine Chile failed to qualify.

POLAND VS SENEGAL

STADIUM - SPARTAK STADIUM

MATCH STATS

POLAND		SENEGAL
11	Total Shots	8
4	Shots on Target	2
3	Corners	3
568	Total Passes	360
9	Total Crosses	11
62	Balls Recovered	55
48	Duels Won	45
8	Fouls Committed	15

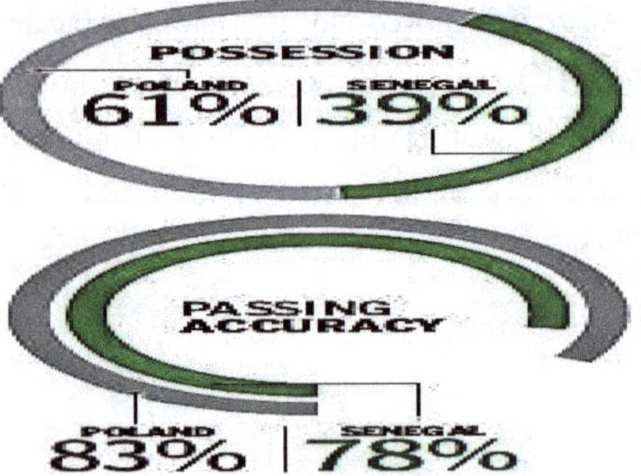

COLOMBIA VS JAPAN

STADIUM - MORDOVIA ARENA

COLOMBIA 1
Quintero 39

JAPAN 2
Kagawa 6-pen, Osako 73

MATCH STATS

COLOMBIA		JAPAN
8	Total Shots	14
3	Shots on Target	5
3	Corners	6
376	Total Passes	594
12	Total Crosses	17
55	Balls Recovered	60
53	Duels Won	69
15	Fouls Committed	9

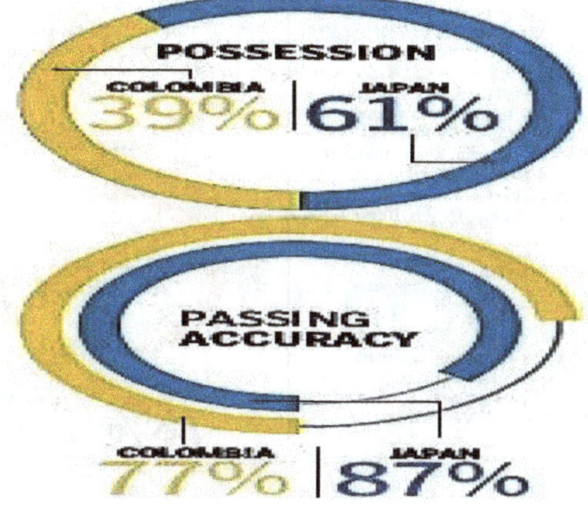

ENGLAND VS TUNISIA

STADIUM - VOLGOGRAD ARENA

It was Kane who won this match for England. It was him who was always there at the right time. He is the optimal striker. The spaces that were created by Kane were very scary

— **Nabil Maaloul**, Tunisia coach

I AM ABSOLUTELY BUZZING, EVERYONE ON THE STAFF IS. IT SHOWS GOOD CHARACTER TO GET THE JOB DONE.

— **Harry Kane**, England striker

26 England's starting XI had an average age of 26 years, 16 days — youngest for the opening WC game since 2002 vs Sweden (25y 207d). The England starting XI had a cumulative total of 248 caps, the lowest by an England starting XI in a tournament since June 1962 (246 caps v Bulgaria).

18.3m The peak audience for the England-Tunisia game, making it Britain's most-watched TV programme of 2018, even beating the Royal Wedding

MATCH STATS

TUNISIA		ENGLAND
6	Total Shots	18
2	Shots on Target	6
2	Corners	7
352	Total Passes	530
4	Total Crosses	22
53	Balls Recovered	52
43	Duels Won	62
14	Fouls Committed	8

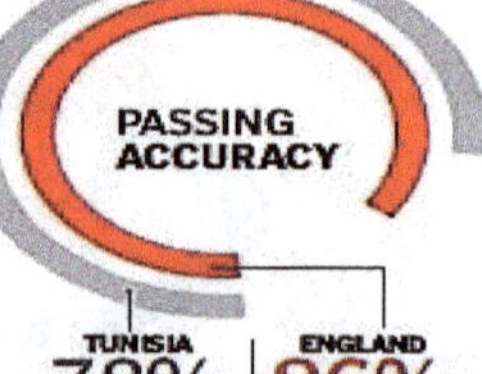

PASSING ACCURACY

TUNISIA 78% | ENGLAND 86%

HOW THEY STAND AFTER ROUND 1

HOW THEY STAND (AFTER ROUND 1)

	P	W	D	L	GD	Pt
Group A						
Russia	1	1	0	0	5	3
Uruguay	1	1	0	0	1	3
Egypt	1	0	0	1	-1	0
S. Arabia	1	0	0	1	-5	0
Group B						
Iran	1	1	0	0	1	3
Portugal	1	0	1	0	0	1
Spain	1	0	1	0	0	1
Morocco	1	0	0	1	-1	0
Group C						
France	1	1	0	0	1	3
Denmark	1	1	0	0	1	3
Australia	1	0	0	1	-1	0
Peru	1	0	0	1	-1	0
Group D						
Croatia	1	1	0	0	2	3
Iceland	1	0	1	0	0	1
Argentina	1	0	1	0	0	1
Nigeria	1	0	0	1	-2	0

	P	W	D	L	GD	Pt
Group E						
Serbia	1	1	0	0	1	3
Brazil	1	0	1	0	0	1
Switzerland	1	0	1	0	0	1
Costa Rica	1	0	0	1	-1	0
Group F						
Sweden	1	1	0	0	1	3
Mexico	1	1	0	0	1	3
S. Korea	1	0	0	1	-1	0
Germany	1	0	0	1	-1	0
Group G						
Belgium	1	1	0	0	3	3
England	1	1	0	0	1	3
Tunisia	1	0	0	1	-1	0
Panama	1	0	0	1	-3	0
Group H						
Japan	1	1	0	0	1	3
Senegal	1	1	0	0	1	3
Poland	1	0	0	1	-1	0
Colombia	1	0	0	1	-1	0

RUSSIA VS EGYPT

STADIUM - S.T. PETERSBURG

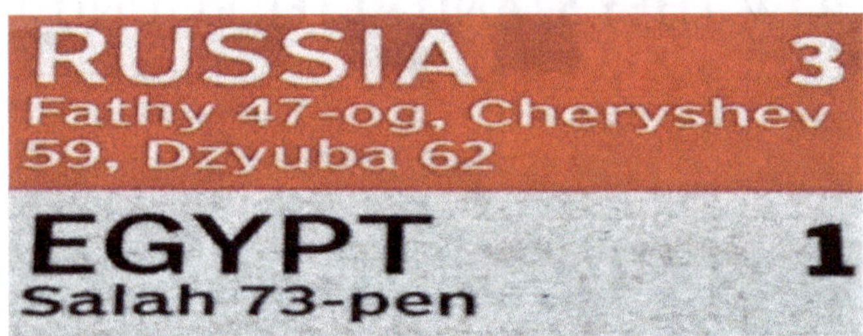

PORTUGAL VS MOROCCO

STADIUM - LUZHNIKI

POR		MOR
10	Total Shots	16
2	Shots on Target	4
5	Corners	7
394	Total Passes	467
1	Yellow Cards	1
105	Distance Covered (km)	107
[illegible]	Fouls Committed	23

URUGUAY VS SAUDI ARABIA

STADIUM - ROSTOV ARENA

MATCH STATS

URUGUAY		SAUDI ARABIA
13	Total Shots	8
3	Shots on Target	2
3	Corners	4
498	Total Passes	550
13	Total Crosses	20
53	Balls Recovered	58
44	Duels Won	38
10	Fouls Committed	13
47%	Possession	53%
85%	Passing Accuracy	87%

URUGUAY 1
Suarez 23
SAUDI ARABIA 0

Smaller Teams Are Surprisingly Good

Now that all the teams have played once, it's time for a first assistant for this World Cup. And right from the outset, we can clearly say this 'This World Cup is really fun.' The football is disciplined and fair, there are no nasty fouls, and so far, the video assistant referee has been working recently, even doing too, maybe three incidents I would have ruled otherwise. But so far, the video assistant referee has fulfilled its task very well. This is the tournament being played at a good level, also because one can see that the so-called smaller teams are surprisingly good. I am not going to say that one of the smaller teams will be the next world champions, but they can be counted on to continue to achieve things against the favourites. Except for Saudi Arabia, so far, no team has disappointed.

This shows that international football is getting more competitive, and that athleticism is increasing. In addition, the organisation of the smaller teams is getting increasingly better, causing problems for some of the favourites. I especially like that there has been fast-paced football, even from teams one had not expected from. This means a rapid changeover from defence to offence, the kind that defending world champions Germany had major problems with against Mexico. I had expected this from Mexico, but other teams are confident playing this style. Even Panama tried it against Belgium.

This World Cup has also shown how important the set-piece situations are in football. These should be practised more.

Set pieces could particularly when it is the big teams helping them live up to their billing. When an opponent lies so deep in its own area, not too many scoring chances can be created. It's a weapon that can decide matches. Just think of England's Harry Kane against Tunisia or Portugal's Cristiano Ronaldo against Spain. This looks to be an emerging trend. When it comes to team unity, Iceland was outstanding. I have rarely before in my life seen a team play as a disciplined collective with a very clear strategy the way Iceland played and maintained for the entire match against Argentina. The 93rd minute was the mirror image of the first second in terms of their system and order.

Danish Players Fly Teammate Home to See New-Born Daughter

Denmark's players clubbed together so defender Jonas Knudsen could fly home on a private jet to see his new-born daughter shortly after their win over Peru in their first match at the World Cup. Knudsen's wife Trine gave birth to a girl several weeks earlier than expected after he had already arrived in Russia; in a gesture of team unity, the players decided to pay for the jet to fly Knudsen home shortly after the 1-0 victory against Peru in group C. "I think you have to remember we are human beings as well as footballers," said goalkeeper Kasper Schmeichel.

FRANCE VS PERU

STADIUM - EKATERINBURG ARENA

MATCH STATS

FRANCE		PERU
12	Total Shots	10
4	Shots on Target	2
391	Total Passes	511
14	Total Crosses	15
65	Balls Recovered	70
74	Duels Won	47
11	Fouls Committed	15
44%	Possession	56%
79%	Passing Accuracy	81%

DENMARK VS AUSTRALIA

STADIUM - SAMARA ARENA

SPAIN VS IRAN

STADIUM - KAZAN ARENA

WHICH CLUBS BENEFIT THE MOST FROM THE WORLD CUP

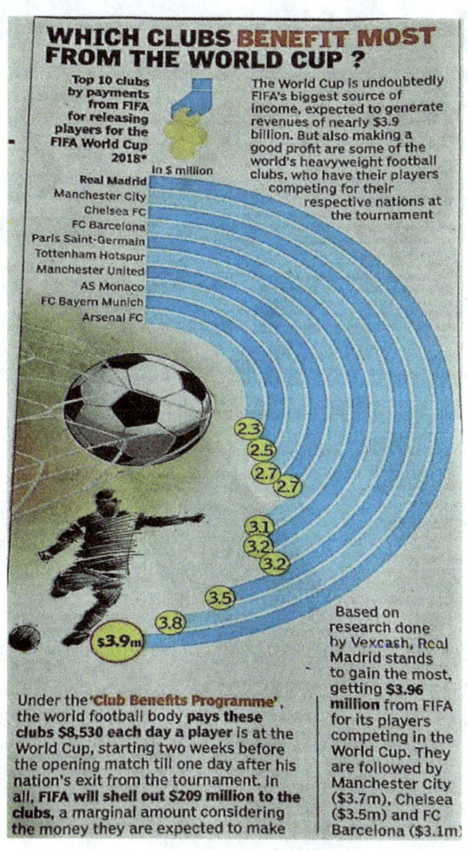

WHICH CLUBS BENEFIT MOST FROM THE WORLD CUP ?

Top 10 clubs by payments from FIFA for releasing players for the FIFA World Cup 2018*

in $ million

Real Madrid	$3.9m
Manchester City	3.8
Chelsea FC	3.5
FC Barcelona	3.2
Paris Saint-Germain	3.2
Tottenham Hotspur	3.1
Manchester United	2.7
AS Monaco	2.7
FC Bayern Munich	2.5
Arsenal FC	2.3

The World Cup is undoubtedly FIFA's biggest source of income, expected to generate revenues of nearly $3.9 billion. But also making a good profit are some of the world's heavyweight football clubs, who have their players competing for their respective nations at the tournament

Under the **'Club Benefits Programme'**, the world football body **pays these clubs $8,530 each day a player** is at the World Cup, starting two weeks before the opening match till one day after his nation's exit from the tournament. In all, **FIFA will shell out $209 million to the clubs**, a marginal amount considering the money they are expected to make

Based on research done by Vexcash, Real Madrid stands to gain the most, getting **$3.96 million** from FIFA for its players competing in the World Cup. They are followed by Manchester City ($3.7m), Chelsea ($3.5m) and FC Barcelona ($3.1m)

BRAZIL VS COSTA RICA

STADIUM - SAINT PETERSBURG

BRAZIL 2
Coutinho 90+1, Neymar 90+7

COSTA RICA 0

BRAZIL		C RICA
22	Total Shots	3
10	Shots on Target	0
9	Corners	1
705	Total Passes	278
28	Total Crosses	8
71	Duels Won	58
58	Balls Recovered	57
11	Fouls Committed	11
72%	Possession	28%
92%	Passing Accuracy	71%

ARGENTINA VS CROATIA

STADIUM - NIZHNY NOVGOROD

MATCH STATS

ARGENTINA		CROATIA
10	Total Shots	14
3	Shots on Target	5
5	Corners	2
500	Total Passes	366
16	Total Crosses	9
47	Balls Recovered	52
61	Duels Won	61
16	Fouls Committed	22

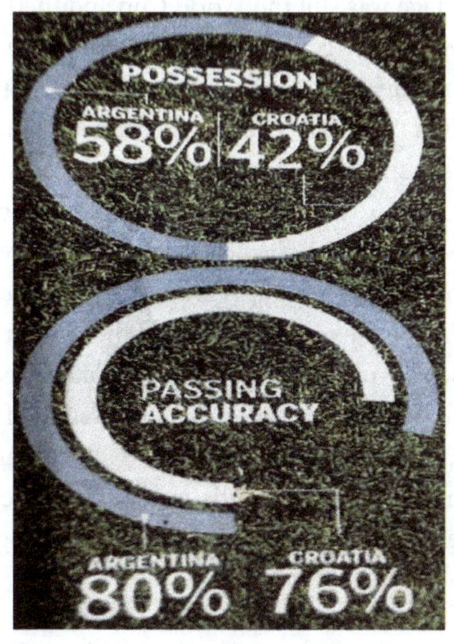

NIGERIA VS ICELAND

STADIUM - VOLGOGRAD ARENA

IT'S CROATIA'S NEW GENERATION

It was the summer of 1998, and the football world was bracing for the usual suspects, Brazil, and Germany, to get into the World Cup semi-finals. But there was a shock in store for fans whose window to world football at that stage was still the World Cup and the Euro. Germany, much like Argentina in Argentina vs Croatia, got mauled by a Croatian team in the quarterfinals 3-0, and we suddenly woke up to the likes of Boban and Davor Suker. A country born out of the breaking of Yugoslavia, Croatia inherited quite a bit of flair that was intrinsic to the East European nation. Tough at the back and smooth in moving forward with an engine like Boban, 1998 could well have been Croatia's year had it not been Lilian Thuram's brace that sunk them in the semi-finals against France. Suker, though, won the golden boot, and his move from Arsenal to Real Madrid a season later was hugely talked about. In terms of silverware, the Golden Generation of 1994-99 didn't win much. Still, they won the hearts of football fans, and rivals knew there was a danger lurking if Croatia were around the corner. There was a similar feeling in the Argentine as well as after the groupings were announced.

We knew what to be expected from Croatia with two of the world's best midfielders—Ivan Rakitic and Luka Modric in their ranks. While Modric is a crucial component of Croatia, Rakitic is one of the less talked about stars who dished out the beautiful game year after year. The duo was impressive in the Euro 2016 and the World Cup qualifiers, but it's not that they had set the stage on fire. But come Argentina, the flair of these two, in addition to the quality of Ivan Persic and Mario Mandzukic, proved a little too much. Marcelo Brozovic was brought in to use his speed to restrict space to Messi. The midfield gave the sense of a well-oiled machine that moved the ball around effortlessly and looked even more incisive against a team that didn't have the wherewithal to respond. Sportske Novoski, a Croatian daily, described the victory as "A magnificent victory to be told by generations to come. It was a rhapsody. Suggesting that the current Croatian generation can make all our dreams come true." Beating Argentina is surely a step towards realising that dream. But winning the odd skirmish soon fades from public memory. What stays are trophies or, at least, being there till the last week of the World Cup? Croatia senses that Modric & Co can go beyond 1998.

BELGIUM VS TUNISIA

STADIUM - SPARTAK STADIUM

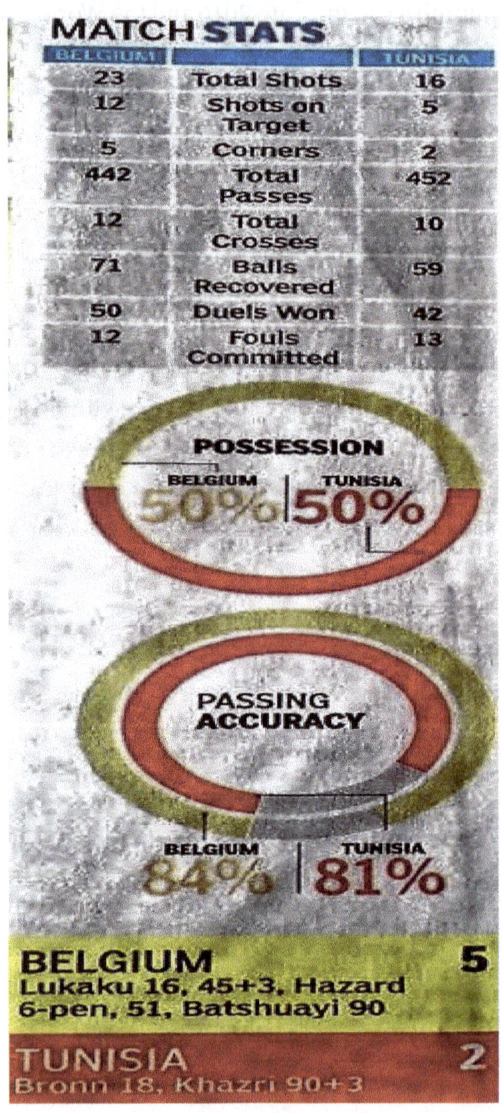

MATCH STATS

BELGIUM		TUNISIA
23	Total Shots	16
12	Shots on Target	5
5	Corners	2
442	Total Passes	452
12	Total Crosses	10
71	Balls Recovered	59
50	Duels Won	42
12	Fouls Committed	13

POSSESSION

BELGIUM 50% | TUNISIA 50%

PASSING ACCURACY

BELGIUM 84% | TUNISIA 81%

BELGIUM 5
Lukaku 16, 45+3, Hazard 6-pen, 51, Batshuayi 90

TUNISIA 2
Bronn 18, Khazri 90+3

SOUTH KOREA VS MEXICO

STADIUM - ROSTOV ARENA

MATCH STATS

KOR		MEX
17	Total Shots	13
6	Shots on Target	5
7	Corners	5
342	Total Passes	477
11	Total Crosses	16
49	Balls Recovered	52
47	Duels Won	67
24	Fouls Committed	7
42%	Possession	58%
81%	Passing Accuracy	87%

SERBIA VS SWITZERLAND

STADIUM - KALININGRAD STADIUM

SERBIA 1
Mitrovic 5

SWITZERLAND 2
Xhaka 52, Shaqiri 90

MATCH STATS

SERBIA		SWITZERLAND
13	Total Shots	20
3	Shots on Target	5
3	Corners	7
309	Total Passes	528
18	Total Crosses	14
59	Balls Recovered	64
72	Duels Won	68
17	Fouls Committed	13
38%	Possession	62%
75%	Passing Accuracy	85%

No Goalless Draws

Goals are the lifeblood of football, and the ongoing World Cup in Russia has already proven to be the liveliest. After Belgium's 5-2 win against Tunisia, the 64-year-old record for the maximum number of matches without a goalless draw in the World Cup has been broken.

There were no goalless draws in all the 26 matches played in the 1954 World Cup in Switzerland, but after Eden Hazard struck the first goal for Belgium in Moscow, this year's tally reached 28 matches. The game has evolved over the years, and one of the reasons why there have been no goalless draws so far can be attributed to the attack-minded formations adopted by managers. Much in vogue today, the 3-5-2 formation, with three defenders and two wing-halves instead of the traditional 4-4-2, allows more gaps in the defence, and teams have been able to find openings in the opponent's backline.

The video assistant referee has played its part with the line calls and penalties often going the way of the team in search of goals. Which 68 goals from 20 games, the goals per-match average for this year's event currently stands at 2.42, less than 2014's 2.7 but more than 2010's 2.3. Interestingly, 1-0 remains the most common result so far, which proves that the cliché' There is no easy game' is not far from the truth.

VAR TAKEAWAYS:

The VAR is proving a constant theme of discussion in the World Cup. It has helped referees to make more correct decisions even though the spontaneity of the game might have taken a hit.

VAR Is No Goal Line Technology (GLT.)

Unlike GLT decisions of a binary nature, goal or no goal, VAR will always have a human person interpreting the rules. So, a reviewed decision may not always receive approval from all parties concerned.

Referees Less Decisive

An argument against VAR is that it has made on-field referees more conservative. They are not ready to make tough calls by themselves and instead would prefer to wait for the VAR to intervene and make it easier for them. So far, four penalties have been awarded after video referrals, showing that on-field referees are banking on the VAR to take control when it comes to game-changing decisions such as penalties.

When VAR Got It Right in Russia:

The first instance of VAR being used to award a penalty was between France and Australia. France's Antoine Griezmann was brought down in the penalty area by Rosh Ridson. Griezmann converted the penalty given after the referee overturned his initial decision in favour of Australia. VAR awarded three more penalties after that in the following games.

The Free Kick Turned into A Penalty

In the match between Egypt and Russia, the referee reviewed a free kick decision in favour of Egypt and decided to award a penalty as it became clear on the referral that the foul on Mohamed Salah had happened inside the area. Salah converted the resultant spot kick.

Offside Goal Disallowed

Saied Ezatolahi of Iran was in an offside position when he scored a goal against Spain. Still, the assistant referee failed to notice it. VAR intervened, and the rest free disallowed the goal, thus reaching the right decision.

Right Player Booked

In the match against France, Peru's Edison Flores was booked incorrectly, as the referee thought it was he who had fouled Nabil Fekir. The booking was correctly changed to Pedro Aquino after VAR informed the referee of his mistake.

Diving Exposed

Brazil's Neymar went theatrically under a challenge from Giancarlo Gonzalez, falling backwards when the defender's arm was on his chest, and a penalty was given at first. But the contact was minimal, and the referee rightfully overturned his decision after watching the replay on screen.

When V.A.R. Might Have Got It Wrong

Denied penalties.

In England's match against Tunisia, Harry Kane had seemingly legitimate penalty claims when he was brought down in the box. Still, the VAR did not advise the referee to investigate the challenges. Similarly, Argentina's Cristian Pavon went down in contact with Birkir Saevarsson of Iceland. However, there was no review as the VAR interpreted that there was no foul on Pavon robbing Argentina of a penalty.

The red card offence went unpunished.

Croatia's Ante Rebic stamped Argentina's Eduardo Salvio on his shin with studs. The referee issued a yellow card, but VAR goes to have intervened to make it a red card, a suitable punishment for an infringement of nature. Still, it did not, and Croatia benefited from that decision as Rebic went on to score the opener in the 3-0 win.

GERMANY VS SWEDEN

STADIUM - FISHT STADIUM

ENGLAND VS PANAMA

STADIUM - NIZHNY NOVGOROD

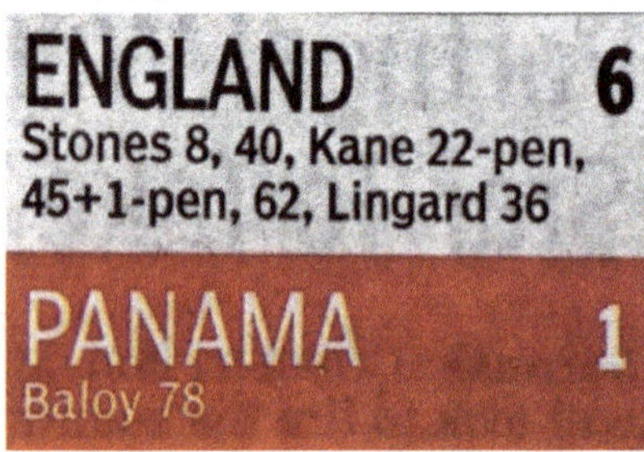

MATCH STATS

ENG		PAN
11	Total Shots	8
7	Shots on Target	2
3	Corners	2
594	Total Passes	396
5	Total Crosses	15
35	Balls Recovered	31
47	Duels Won	42
13	Fouls	13

JAPAN VS SENEGAL

STADIUM – EKATERINBURG

JAPAN 2
Inui 34, Honda 78

SENEGAL 2
Mane 11, Wague 71

JAPAN		SENEGAL
7	Total Shots	15
3	Shots on Target	7
2	Corners	5
464	Total Passes	339
8	Total Crosses	22
50	Duels Won	53
8	Fouls	15
57%	Possession	43%
79%	Passing	76%

Leo got crafted in chocolate.

When Moscow confectioners found out Lionel Messi would be celebrating his birthday during the World Cup, they decided he needed a given that measured up, a life-size chocolate sculpture in his likeness.

A team of five workers at Moscow's Altufyevo confectionery worked for nearly a week to carve a sculpture in 60 KG of chocolate to mark the striker's 31st birthday. Chief confectioner Daria Malkina said she had been in touch with Messi. He is represented as handing in this culture, which will be mounted on a birthday cake. "We will give Lionel Messi to Lionel Messi," she said.

Tidiest supporters' cleanest stadiums

Once Senegal finished their match against Japan at the Ekaterinburg Arena, the stadium might have become the cleanest one in Russia, going by the history of the fan base of both teams. After the first round of matches, fans of Japan and Senegal were in the news for their efforts to clean up the stadiums before leaving.

It might be my last World Cup, says Pogba.

France midfielder Paul Pogba has said the finals in Russia might be his last World Cup, but we hope he will be fit for more. “It might be my last World Cup,” the player, 25, said ahead of the game against Denmark. France has already qualified for the last 16 and will secure the top spot if they avoid defeat. “I am realistic; we don’t know if I’ll be called up; maybe other players will be better than me,” added Pogba.

URUGUAY VS RUSSIA

STADIUM - SAMARA ARENA

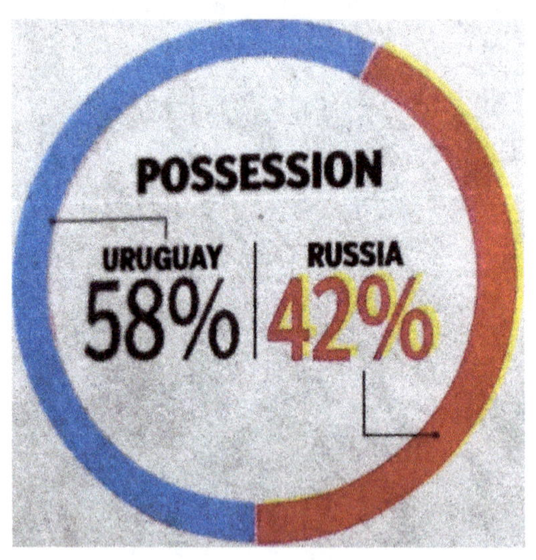

EGYPT VS SAUDI ARABIA

STADIUM - VOLGOGRAD ARENA

POLAND VS COLOMBIA

STADIUM: KAZAN ARENA

Salt, pepper, and vinegar

French players have fresh memories of Denmark coach Age Hareide criticising them before the World Cup. A month ago, Hareide told a Danish newspaper the France team his players will face was "nothing special" and lacked players who were true leaders, and suggested Paul Pogba was too focused on hairstyles. "My players can read; they can listen," France coach Didier Deschamps said. When asked if the comments for the spice of the game at the Luzhniki Stadium, the French coach replied, "Salt, pepper, vinegar, whatever you want."

DENMARK VS FRANCE

STADIUM - LUZHNIKI STADIUM

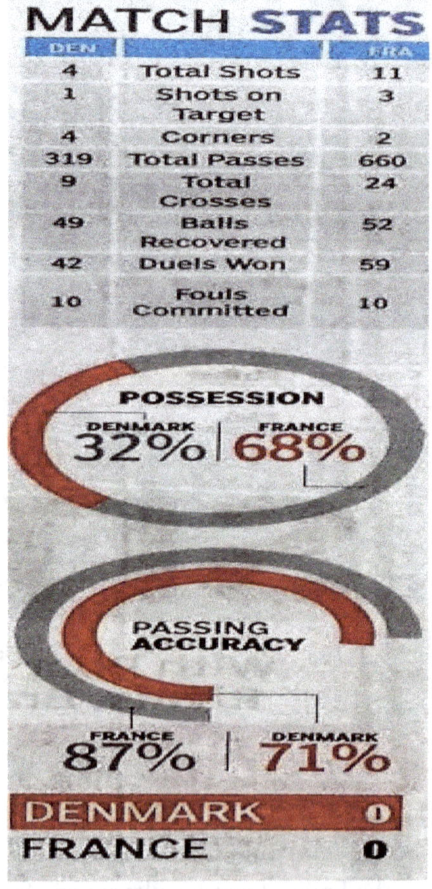
MATCH STATS

DEN		FRA
4	Total Shots	11
1	Shots on Target	3
4	Corners	2
319	Total Passes	660
9	Total Crosses	24
49	Balls Recovered	52
42	Duels Won	59
10	Fouls Committed	10

AUSTRALIA VS PERU

STADIUM - FISHT STADIUM

MATCH STATS

AUS		PER
14	Total Shots	4
2	Shots on Target	3
8	Corners	3
524	Total Passes	411
26	Total Crosses	4
56	Balls Recovered	53
55	Duels Won	56
14	Fouls Committed	12
57%	Possession	43%
87%	Pass Accuracy	80%

IRAN VS PORTUGAL

STADIUM - MORDOVIA ARENA

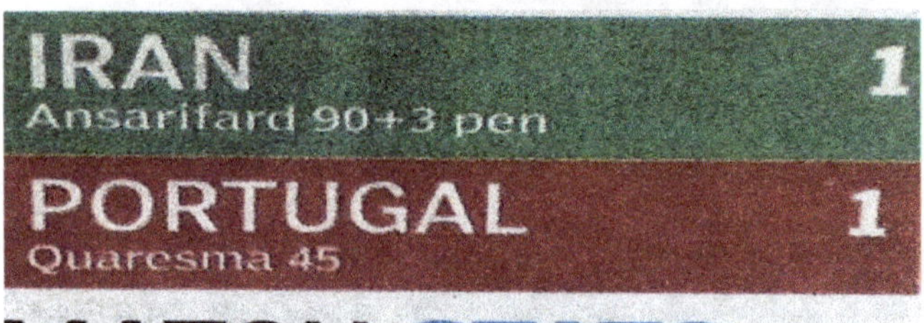

MATCH STATS

IRAN		PORTUGAL
7	Total Shots	14
2	Shots on Target	4
1	Corners	5
212	Total Passes	608
9	Total Crosses	19
59	Balls Recovered	54
48	Duels Won	56
16	Fouls Committed	11
27%	Possession	73%
65%	Passing Accuracy	87%

SPAIN VS MOROCCO

STADIUM - KALININGRAD STADIUM

SPAIN 2
Isco 19, Aspas 90+1

MOROCCO 2
Boutaib 14, En-Nesyri 81

MATCH STATS

SPAIN		MOROCCO
18	Total Shots	6
5	Shots on Target	3
7	Corners	1
740	Total Passes	243
21	Total Crosses	7
47	Balls Recovered	50
54	Duels Won	44
5	Fouls Committed	17
75%	Possession	25%
92%	Passing Accuracy	77%

Uruguay, the master of no-nonsense

Uruguay never had it so smooth, not since 1954. In Switzerland, the most decorated South American footballing nation won back-to-back games in the group stage, and that too handsomely. In 1954, opening with a 2-0 victory over Czechoslovakia, the Uruguayans walloped Scotland 7-0. They were sitting pretty with six points from two games, both secured with the slenderest of margins, against Saudi Arabia and

Egypt, in not quite their adorable trademark style. Then, captained by Diego Godin, Uruguay went one better. In the last group game, they got the better of hosts Russia 3-0.

It seems happy times are right back for Luis Suarez, famous across the world for scoring remarkable goals and for biting the opponent. The Uruguayans' Best performance in recent times came in South Africa in 2010 when they finished fourth, and Diego Forlan claimed the golden ball. With the storied football tradition, Uruguay, more often than not, flatter to deceive with their robust style and lack of flair. Throwing up a couple of quality players of exceptional ability in every generation. Similar to their next-door neighbours Argentina and Paraguay.

MEXICO VS SWEDEN

STADIUM – EKATERINBURG

MATCH STATS

MEXICO		SWEDEN
20	Total Shots	15
3	Shots on Target	5
7	Corners	3
473	Total Passes	240
22	Total Crosses	9
53	Balls Recovered	52
56	Duels Won	63
14	Fouls Committed	11
67%	Possession	33%
83%	Passing Accuracy	61%

MEXICO 0

SWEDEN 3

Augustinsson 50, Granqvist 62-Pen, E Alvarez OG

15 Seconds when Mexico's Jesús Gallardo was shown a yellow card in this game – the fastest at the World Cup.

7 Mexico full-back Edson Alvarez scored the seventh own-goal of this tournament – more than in any World Cup.

SOUTH KOREA VS GERMANY

STADIUM - KAZAN ARENA

MATCH STATS

S KOREA		GERMANY
12	Total Shots	28
5	Shots on Target	6
3	Corners	9
246	Total Passes	697
6	Total Crosses	33
58	Balls Recovered	58
43	Duels Won	68
16	Fouls Committed	7

ICELAND VS CROATIA

STADIUM - ROSTOV ARENA

NIGERIA VS ARGENTINA

STADIUM - NIZHNY NOVGOROD

NIGERIA 1
Moses 51-pen
ARGENTINA 2
Messi 14, Rojo 86

MATCH STATS

NIGERIA		ARGENTINA
9	Total Shots	8
3	Shots on Target	4
7	Corners	5
286	Total Passes	572
9	Total Crosses	18
50	Balls Recovered	50
68	Duels Won	72
20	Fouls Committed	15
33%	Possession	67%
66%	Passing Accuracy	82%

Diego Maradona is Argentina's biggest fan and distraction.

He danced, he dozed, he prayed, he gave a double middle finger salute to spectators, and then, when it was all over, he was helped out of his chair and out of the stadium. Maradona's performance in the stands was as eye-catching as was the one produced on the field by Lionel Messi on Argentina's 2-1 win over Nigeria, which spared them from early elimination. Maradona might be Argentina's number-one fan at the World Cup. Still, he is also proving to be an unwanted and sometimes embarrassing distraction, increasingly casting a shadow on the team.

ENGLAND VS BELGIUM

STADIUM - KALININGRAD STADIUM

MATCH STATS

ENGLAND		BELGIUM
8	Total Shots	7
2	Shots on Target	4
7	Corners	2
469	Total Passes	547
18	Total Crosses	6
54	Balls Recovered	51
61	Duels Won	58
11	Fouls Committed	14

PANAMA VS TUNISIA

STADIUM - MORDOVIA ARENA

MATCH STATS

PANAMA		TUNISIA
8	Total Shots	11
4	Shots on Target	6
0	Corners	6
275	Total Passes	618
5	Total Crosses	18
54	Balls Recovered	56
53	Duels Won	63
18	Fouls Committed	19

Fearful favourites, upbeat underdogs

There is an insurrection in the world of football. And it's not just that holders Germany were knocked out before the knockouts began. Even Argentina, Spain, and Brazil - all card-holding members of football royalty - what made to sweat and shiver by the teams of lesser pedigree. Iran, South Korea, Nigeria, and even Saudi Arabia had their moments in the ongoing 2018 World Cup in Russia. They earned points and prestige. But more importantly, they made matches most utterly unpredictable. Now only 16 teams remain. The knockouts are about to begin. Get ready for the unexpected.

TALKING POINT:

VAR crimes

Football is polarised over the video assistant referee (V.A.R.). Undeniably, VAR has minimised errors on the field. But any neutral football fan who saw its usage in Iran vs Portugal, Spain vs Morocco, and Serbia vs Switzerland matches will admit that it is still very much a work in progress.

It's Time for Others to Back Messi Up

The initial drama is over. Defending champions are out of the World Cup. The best 16 have progressed to the knockouts. It's time for real football. Fighters of the highest order will survive. It's not only about skills and strategies anymore; it's also about nerves. The one who blinks first will fall by the wayside. The knockouts generally promise gripping action. This time, it's a bit too much to begin with. France against Argentina and Uruguay vs Portugal are clashes of heavyweights, the kind you normally expect at a later stage of the competition. The teams have had contrasting parts to the last 16. On this day, they start from scratch. Nobody starts as favourites.

Iran's Hero

Iran's 25-year-old goalkeeper Alireza Beiranvand, who pulled off an improbable penalty save to deny the imperious Ronaldo, has been one of the most outstanding performances of World Cup 2018. The story of his life is equally amazing. Beiranvand was born in a nomadic family. He spent his early childhood grazing sheep and developed of fondness for football. At a young age, he ran away from home to Teheran to pursue his passion. Times were tough. He once slept outside of a football club's office door. "When I woke in the morning, I noticed the coins people had dropped for me. They had thought I was a beggar! Well, I had a delicious breakfast for the first time in a long while," said the goalkeeper, who also made a bunch of spectacular saves against Spain, told the Guardian newspaper.

As he struggled to make his mark as a player, Beiranvand worked at a dress-making factory, a carwash, and a pizza shop to eke out a living. He has since developed into a world-class goalie with a penchant for long throws like the Russian great Lev Yashin. Beiranvand has no place in Iran's famous Persepolis Club and is among the club's top earners.

TEAMS QUALIFIED FOR THE ROUND OF 16

1. URUGUAY
2. RUSSIA
3. SPAIN
4. PORTUGAL
5. FRANCE
6. DENMARK
7. CROATIA
8. ARGENTINA
9. BRAZIL
10. SWITZERLAND
11. SWEDEN
12. MEXICO
13. BELGIUM
14. ENGLAND
15. COLOMBIA
16. JAPAN

ROUND OF 16

ARGENTINA VS FRANCE

STADIUM - KAZAN ARENA

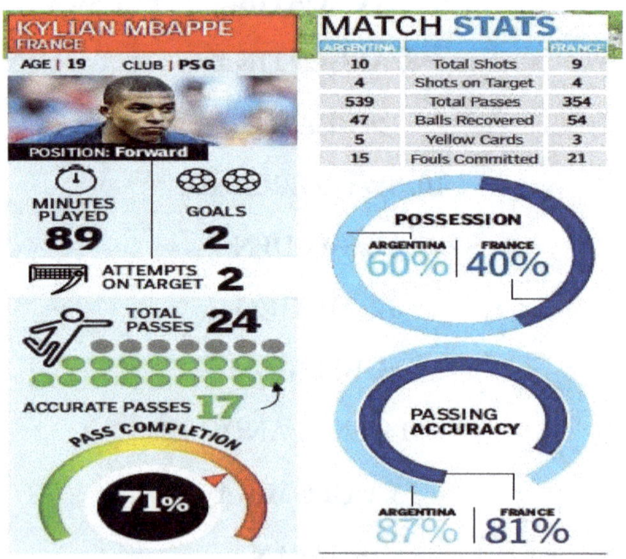

SPAIN VS RUSSIA

STADIUM - FISHT STADIUM

SPAIN 1
Ignashevich 12-og

RUSSIA 1
Dzyuba 41-pen

PENALTY SHOOTOUT

SPAIN		RUSSIA	
Iniesta	⚽	Smolov	⚽
Pique	⚽	Ignashevich	⚽
Koke	✕	Golovin	⚽
Ramos	⚽	Cheryshev	⚽
Aspas	✕		

MATCH STATS

SPAIN		RUSSIA
25	Total Shots	7
9	Shots on Target	1
6	Corners	5
1114	Total Passes	290
27	Total Crosses	12
55	Balls Recovered	61
1	Yellow Cards	2
5	Fouls Committed	19

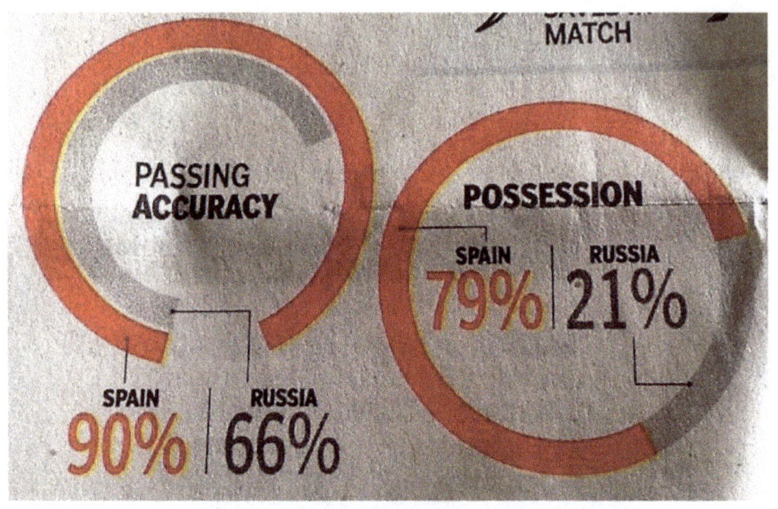

Messi and Ronaldo walk into the sunset.

It happened one night. Within six hours and 200 km apart, Lionel Messi and Cristiano Ronaldo said goodbye to the World Cup, in all likelihood never to return. From being the cynosure of all eyes, isolation, we'll be their next address, their journey to be the greatest of all time has ended abruptly. At the Kazan arena, Messi looked on hopelessly as a certain 19-year-old French kid pulled the carpet from under Argentina's feet, sending the message that it was time to abdicate. Deep down south of Russia on the shores of the Black Sea, Ronaldo's galley failed to weather one more storm and sank. Iran first plugged a hole in the portside, and the Cavani typhoon finally called the ship down to the ocean bed.

BRAZIL VS MEXICO

STADIUM - LUZHNIKI STADIUM

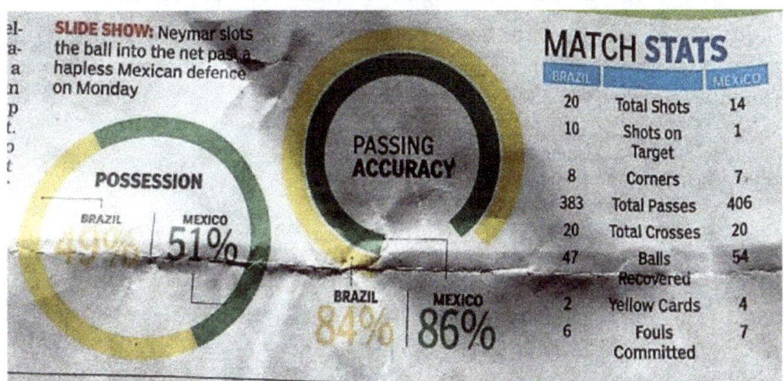

MATCH STATS

BRAZIL		MEXICO
20	Total Shots	14
10	Shots on Target	1
8	Corners	7
383	Total Passes	406
20	Total Crosses	20
47	Balls Recovered	54
2	Yellow Cards	4
6	Fouls Committed	7

So long Iniesta farewell Tiki - Taka

Passed, passed, passed, and passed away.

Even Andres Iniesta how says, "Sometimes the endings are not how you dreamed them. "I Spain fell to the Roulette rather unheroically, Iniesta, 34, decided to bring down the curtains on the career that had reached Himalayan heights long before he touched 30. Winning the first La Liga title at 20 and the champions league year later, Iniesta's first continental title came when he was just 24. The Luis Aragones—led Spain dumped their underachiever's tag to win the Euro 2008, with

Xavi - Iniesta combination taking its rightful place in world football.

Croatia will not stop here: Coach.

Zlatko Dalic said he wanted Asia's World Cup adventure to continue past the quarterfinals after his team secured a last-eight spot with a dramatic penalty shootout victory over Denmark. The Croats won 3-2 on penalties after a tense 1-1 draw to set up a clash with hosts Russia. But Dalic said his team, who have been tipped for World Cup glory, want to go much further. "We have come so far, but we don't intend to stop here," Dalic said. His team "played for the result," and he was unconcerned about the performance. The victory came after three penalty saves from keeper Danijel Subasic in the shootout, the first to do that since Portugal's Ricardo against England in 2006. "You have to earn your luck, and the lads earned theirs," he said. "Without luck, you can't do anything in life."

Thierry Henry's Influence

There was a sense of déjà vu around Kevin De Bruyne's searing run down the middle that shattered Japan's dreams. For once, your mind veered to those Premier League nights in the first decade of the 2000s when a certain Thierry Henry was doing the same for Arsenal at the theatre of Highbury. Years have rolled by, and Henry has left the shores and is now an apprentice coach under Roberto Martinez on the Belgian side. An apprentice is probably an understatement; the French legend works with the Belgian attacking line, trying to infuse an instinct that made Arsenal such a loved team in those years. Not that De Bruyne has learnt the art of those galloping runs from Henry; he has done it over the years for the clubs he has played for—be it Wolfsburg or Manchester City. But the attack-at-all-cost football that this Belgian side plays may have something to do with Henry.

QUARTERFINALS

GAME 1

Who can stop Mbappe Express?

Uruguay vs France | July 6, 7.30pm | Nizhny Novgorod

HEAD TO HEAD: Uruguay have lost to France just once in eight meetings. The South Americans won their last encounter 1-0, a friendly in June 2013

FRANCE
Fifa Rank: 7
WC Best: Winners 1998
In 2014: Reached last eight

Road to quarters: Beat Australia 2-1, Peru 1-0, drew with Denmark 0-0, beat Argentina 4-3
Strength: Packed with A-listers in all departments
Weakness: Conceded three goals against Argentina, which suggests a vulnerability in the Les Bleus defence
Watch out for: Paul Pogba. This could be his day
Will be missed: Dependable medio Blaise Matuidi serving out a one-match suspension
Coach: Didier Deschamps. His second WC finals as France manager. Playing under his guidance in WC2014, France lost to eventual winners Germany 1-0 in quarters

MOST GOALS
Mbappe 3 | Cavani 3

MOST CLEARANCES
Varane 26 | Godin 19

URUGUAY
Rank: 14
WC Best: Winners (1930, 1950)
In 2014: Reached pre-quarters

Road to quarters: Beat Egypt 1-0, Saudi Arabia 1-0, Russia 3-0, Portugal 2-1
Strength: Speedy attacks. Sound defence marshalled by Diego Godin and Jose Gimenez. Have conceded only one goal in four games
Weakness: Lack the overall quality and depth of their opponent
Watch out for: The goal-hungry and incisive forward Luis Suarez
Doubtful: In-form striker Edinson Cavani has a swollen left calf
Coach: Oscar Tabarez is making a fourth World Cup appearance (1990, 2010 and 2014), more than any other manager in this World Cup

WHAT THE NUMBERS REVEAL

1 In WC2018, Uruguay made their third appearance in a row. This is France's sixth unbroken appearance, their longest ever

2 Uruguay's first appearance in a WC quarter-final since 2010, when they beat Ghana 4-2 on penalties following a 1-1 draw

3 France are unbeaten in their last nine WC matches against South American sides (five wins, four draws). Les Bleus kept a clean sheet in seven

4 France have advanced on four of the last five occasions they reached the quarters, the only exception being a 0-1 defeat against Germany in 2014

GAME 2

When World No. 2 takes on World No. 3

Brazil vs Belgium | July 6, 11.30pm | Kazan

HEAD TO HEAD: Four previous meetings. Belgium won the first way back in 1963. Brazil won the other three. In their only WC face-off, in 2002, the South Americans won 2-0

BRAZIL
Rank: 2
WC Best: Five-time champions (1958, 1962, 1970, 1994 & 2002)
In 2014: Finished 4th

Road to quarters: Drew with Switzerland 1-1, beat Costa Rica 2-0, Serbia 2-0, Mexico 2-0
Strength: Complete package. Rock-solid defence. Gifted forward line
Weakness: Untested when a goal behind
Watch out for: Neymar. He might score goals or win an Oscar
Will be missed: Casemiro. The holding midfielder from Real Madrid is serving card suspension
Coach: Tite. Under him, Brazil have triumphed in 80% of their 25 matches

MOST GOALS
Lukaku 4 | Coutinho & Neymar 2 each

MOST CLEARANCES
Boyata 12 | Silva 20

BELGIUM
Rank: 3
WC Best: Finished 4th (1986)
In 2014: Reached quarters

Road to quarters: Beat Panama 3-0, Tunisia 5-2, England 1-0, Japan 3-2
Strength: Versatile attacking team. 12 goals scored by 8 different players, no team has more scorers
Weakness: Aging defender Vincent Kompany has looked shaky
Watch out for: Kevin De Bruyne, the multi-purpose medio who plays for Man City
Injury concerns: Niggles aside, the squad is up and running
Coach: Roberto Martínez. The Spanish manager is the first non-Belgian to lead the Red Devils in a World Cup since Doug Livingstone in 1954

WHAT THE NUMBERS REVEAL

1 Belgium have lost three of their last four World Cup meetings against South American opposition

2 Brazil are playing the quarters for the seventh successive World Cup. They've only gone out twice at this stage (vs France in 2006 and vs the Netherlands in 2010)

3 The Selecao have been knocked out of the World Cup by a European side in each of the last three tournaments (vs France in 2006, Netherlands in 2010 and Germany in 2014)

4 Belgium have reached consecutive World Cup quarters for the first time

5 Brazil are unbeaten in their last 15 matches (11 wins, 4 draws), conceding just three goals

6 Belgium are unbeaten in their last 23 matches (18 wins, 5 draws), the longest run among the eight quarterfinalists

GAME 3 | England vs Sweden | July 7, 7.30pm | Samara

HEAD TO HEAD: The two have met 24 times. England have won eight, Sweden seven with nine draws. In WC, the two collided in 2002 (1-1) and 2006 (2-2)

ENGLAND
Fifa Rank: 12
WC Best: Winners (1966)
In 2014: Group stage exit

Road to quarters: Beat Tunisia 2-1, Panama 6-1. Lost to Belgium 0-1. Beat Colombia on penalties, extra-time score 1-1

Strength: A young squad playing without the baggage and burden of past. Apart from forward Harry Kane, defenders John Stones and Kieran Trippier have excelled in attacking roles

Weakness: Can wilt under pressure, as evident against Colombia

Watch out for: Can Kane get a seventh?

Doubtful: Dele Alli, Ashley Young, Jamie Vardy — all have injury issues

Coach: Gareth Southgate. England have lost only one match under him

SWEDEN
Fifa Rank: 24
WC Best: Runners-up (1958)
In 2014: Did not qualify

Road to quarters: Beat South Korea 1-0. Lost to Germany 1-2. Beat Mexico 3-0, Switzerland 1-0

Strength: Hard to break down. Functions as all-for-one, one-for-all unit

Weakness: Lacks individual brilliance and creativity

Watch out for: Emil Forsberg, the midfielder who makes the team tick

Will be missed: Sebastian Larsson and Lustig, both are serving one match suspension after receiving two yellow cards

Coach: Janne Andersson has led Sweden to their first World Cup finals since 2006, beating Italy 1-0 on aggregate in a play-off

MOST GOALS	
Kane	Granqvist
6	2

MOST CLEARANCES	
Stones	Granqvist, Lustig
15	24

WHAT THE NUMBERS REVEAL

1 England have reached the World Cup quarters for the first time since 2006

2 11 of Sweden's last 14 goals at WC have been scored in the second half, including five of their six goals at this tournament

3 Harry Kane has scored with each of his six shots on target, including three penalties. The last player to score three from penalties in WC was Bulgaria's Hristo Stoichkov in 1994

4 Sweden striker Marcus Berg has takes 13 shots without scoring, the most by any player yet to score in Russia

Granqvist

GAME 4 | **Can Russian roulette claim another victim?**

Croatia vs Russia | July 7, 11.30pm | Sochi

HEAD TO HEAD: The two have played each other thrice. Two games ended goalless. Croatia won the third face-off in November 2015, claiming a 3-1 victory

CROATIA
Rank: 20
WC Best: 3rd in 1998
In 2014: Group stage exit

Road to quarters: Beat Nigeria 2-0, Argentina 3-0, Iceland 2-1, Denmark on penalties after finishing 1-1

Strength: Abounds in high-class midfield talent such as Luka Modric, Ivan Rakitic, Mateo Kovacic. Solid defence too

Weakness: The hard-working Mario Mandzukic aside, perhaps needs more finishing prowess

Watch out for: Goalie Danijel Subasic. He could be needed in another shoot-out

Will be missed: Everybody's available

Coach: Zlatko Dalic was asked to take charge just two days before their 'must-win' game against Ukraine in the 2018 qualifiers. He guided Croatia to a 2-0 win & into the playoffs

RUSSIA
Rank: 70
WC Best: 4th in 1966 (as USSR)
In 2014: Group stage exit

Road to quarters: Beat Saudi Arabia 5-0, Egypt 3-1, lost to Uruguay 0-3, beat Spain on penalties, extra-time score 1-1

Strength: Obdurate rearguard. Creativity of midfielder Aleksandr Golovin. Home fan support. Goalkeeper Igor Akinfeev

Weakness: Lacks bolt

Watch out for: Roman Zobrin, whose distribution the team relies on

Will be missed: Midfielder Yuri Zhirkov has a calf muscle inflammation

Coach: Stanislav Cherchesev is the first to represent Russia both as a coach and a player

MOST GOALS	
Modric	Cheryshev, Dzyuba
2	3

MOST CLEARANCES	
Vida	Ignashevich
20	31

WHAT THE NUMBERS REVEAL

1 Russia have reached the quarters for the first time since the breakup of the Soviet Union

2 Croatia won their only other WC quarter-final, defeating Germany in 1998 on their way to that year's semis, where they were eliminated

3 The last five host nations to feature in a World Cup quarter-final have all progressed to the semis (Italy 1990, France 1998, South Korea 2002, Germany 2006 and Brazil 2014)

4 Croatia have only lost one of their seven World Cup matches against fellow European opposition. They have won five times and drawn one

5 10 of Croatia's last 12 World Cup goals have come in the second halves of their games

Source: opta

Cheryshev

Modric

YOU BET | NAME THE FINALISTS | Brazil/England 5/1 | France/England 11/2

William Hill

TEAMS QUALIFIED FOR QUARTERFINALS

1. URUGUAY
2. RUSSIA
3. FRANCE
4. CROATIA
5. SWEDEN
6. ENGLAND
7. BELGIUM
8. BRAZIL

THE UNSUNG HEROES

Guy Stephan: Assistant Coach, France

France coach Didier Deschamps and Stephan, his trusted assistant for the past six years, have known each other since 2000. "People like him are rare," FFF President Noel Le Graet said of Stephan, who is looked upon as a father figure in the Les Bleus Camp. "Three words are not enough to describe him: he is faithful, honest, efficient, and intelligent," Le Graet added.

Yury Zhirkov: Midfielder, Russia

When fans reflect on the host nation's memorable campaign, Denis Cheryshev, Aleksander Golovin, and Igor Akinfeev are likely to be the first names that will spring to mind. However, veteran Yury Zhirkov has also played his part, most notably batting on for the famous round of 16 win over Spain with a leg injury. "Even before the game, I felt pain in the Achilles' tendon," he revealed.

Maximiliano Pereira: Defender, Uruguay

The veteran defender is as good an example as you will get of a player having a positive impact on the team, even if you may not have had a single minute of playing time. La Celeste captain Diego Godin said, "He's been important to the team for many years and continues to be."

Allan Russell: Attacking Coach, England.

Manager Southgate would attribute his team's efficiency to one man, in particular, attacking coach Allan Russell. "There are very few people who actually work at this level of detail about it," said Southgate.

Daniel Ekvall: Sports Psychology Advisor, Sweden

If you've become an admirer of Sweden's unity and mental strength, that's largely down to the excellent work of their sports psychology advisor Daniel Ekvall says. "From what the players say in those, I create a mental plan for the upcoming match."

Iva Olivari: Team Manager, Croatia

Regardless of how far Croatia goes, Russia 2018 will always be special for the team manager, Iva Olivari, as she is the first woman to sit on the bench for the national team at the World Cup. Employed with the Croatian Football Federation since 1992, Olivari, A former National tennis champion in under 14 level, manages the squad's logistics and travel plans.

Cleber Xavier: Assistant Coach, Brazil

Seventeen years is how long Cleber Xavier has worked with Brazil boss Tite. There is no stronger indication of Tite's trust and respect for his coaching staff than this stat.

Axel Witsel, Midfielder, Belgium

Versatility is a trade that would endear any player to his coach, and it is what makes Witsel such a vital cog in the Belgium set-up, where he occupies a deep-lying midfield role. "It is my nature to be calm," he says. "It helps us on the pitch when facing tense moments, and I try to convey this serenity to the rest of the players when they need it."

URUGUAY VS FRANCE

STADIUM - NIZHNY NOVGOROD

MATCH STATS

URUGUAY		FRANCE
11	Total Shots	11
4	Shots on Target	2
4	Corners	3
311	Total Passes	516
25	Total Crosses	17
59	Balls Recovered	56
2	Yellow Cards	2
17	Fouls Committed	15

Kempes Offers to Coach Argentina

Hot on the heels of Diego Maradona, another Argentine World Cup winner has thrown his hat into the ring to become the next national team coach. Jorge Sampaoli may still be resisting pressure to resign, but Mario Kempes has said he wants to take over. "Of course!" he said when asked by ESPN if he would be interested in the job. "There's a lot I have work to do, but there is enough time to come up with a good project to tackle a very interesting challenge, and I'm sure it would win," said Kempes.

BELGIUM VS BRAZIL

STADIUM - KAZAN ARENA

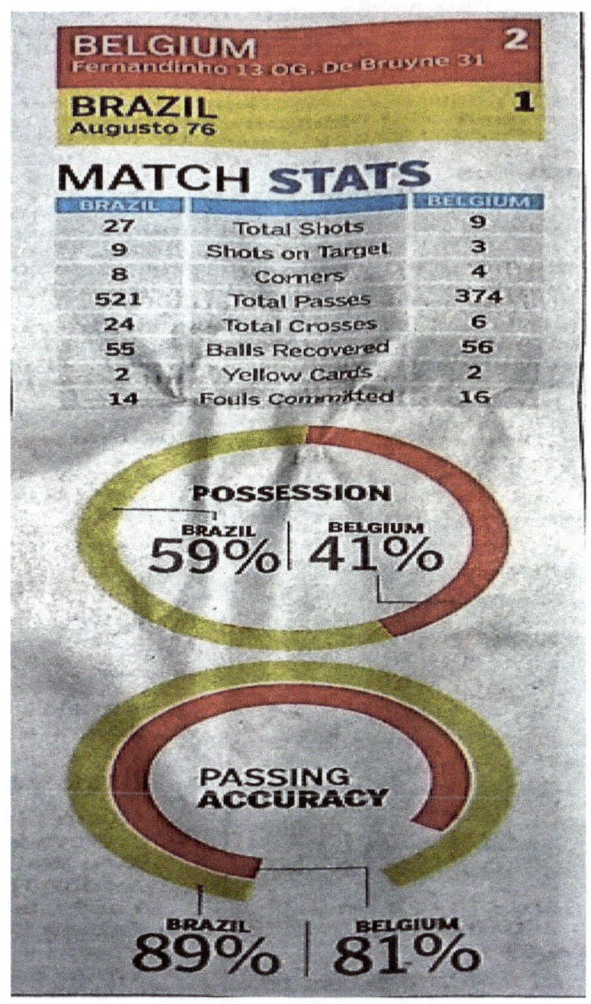

BELGIUM 2
Fernandinho 13 OG, De Bruyne 31

BRAZIL 1
Augusto 76

MATCH STATS

BRAZIL		BELGIUM
27	Total Shots	9
9	Shots on Target	3
8	Corners	4
521	Total Passes	374
24	Total Crosses	6
55	Balls Recovered	56
2	Yellow Cards	2
14	Fouls Committed	16

POSSESSION
BRAZIL 59% | BELGIUM 41%

PASSING ACCURACY
BRAZIL 89% | BELGIUM 81%

SWEDEN VS ENGLAND

STADIUM - SAMARA ARENA

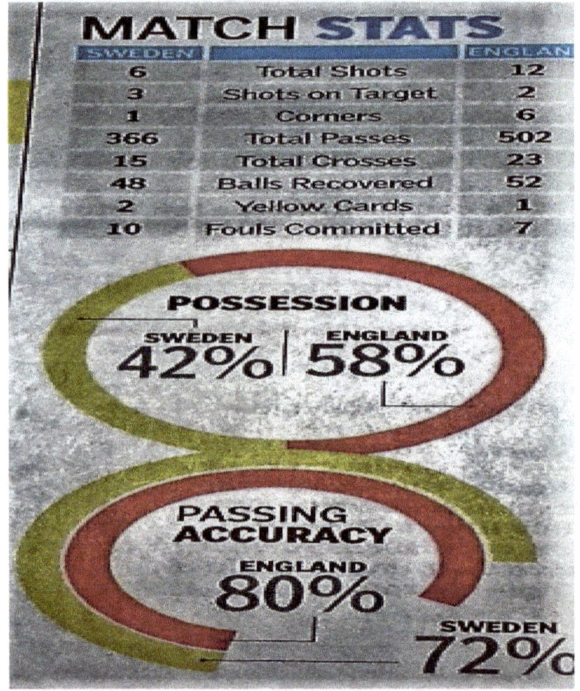

MATCH STATS

SWEDEN		ENGLAN
6	Total Shots	12
3	Shots on Target	2
1	Corners	6
366	Total Passes	502
15	Total Crosses	23
48	Balls Recovered	52
2	Yellow Cards	1
10	Fouls Committed	7

POSSESSION

SWEDEN 42% | ENGLAND 58%

PASSING ACCURACY

ENGLAND 80%

SWEDEN 72%

How Martinez Outfoxed Tite:

Extra defensive cover

All throughout, Belgium had played a 3 - 4 - 2 - 1 formation. Against Brazil, Martinez went for four men at the back, with Thomas Meunier dropping back as a right fullback, giving them a more defensive cushion in a conventional 4 - 3 - 3 set-up. It worked, considering Brazil preferred to attack down the left with Marcelo advancing forward.

De Bruyne as falls No.9

Kevin De Bruyne had played as a deep-lying playmaker. But Martinez surprised everyone by employing him as a false No.9 in a three-man forward line with Eden Hazard and Romelu Lukaku. De Bruyne benefited from the advanced role and went on to score a breakaway second goal set up by Lukaku.

Lukaku - The right choice

Martinez repeated a tactical masterstroke he had pulled off as an Everton Manager against Arsenal in 2014. Lukaku, stationed on the right, wreaked havoc in Everton's 3 - 0 win. Taking a cue, Martinez played Lukaku on the right against Brazil, and the striker repeatedly received the ball on a vast open field on the right vacated by Marcelo. The Brazilian centre-back Miranda was often seen struggling to keep up with the physicality of the Belgian, who created the second goal after a fantastic dribble from his own half before setting up De Bruyne.

Not buckling under pressure.

Towards the end, when Brazil started throwing everything into attack, Martinez switched to 5 men at the back-introducing Thomas Vermaelen for Chadli. Hazard played more centrally in a 5 - 3 - 1 - 1 to gather the clearances, hold a play and frustrate the Brazilians.

RUSSIA VS CROATIA

STADIUM - FISHT STADIUM

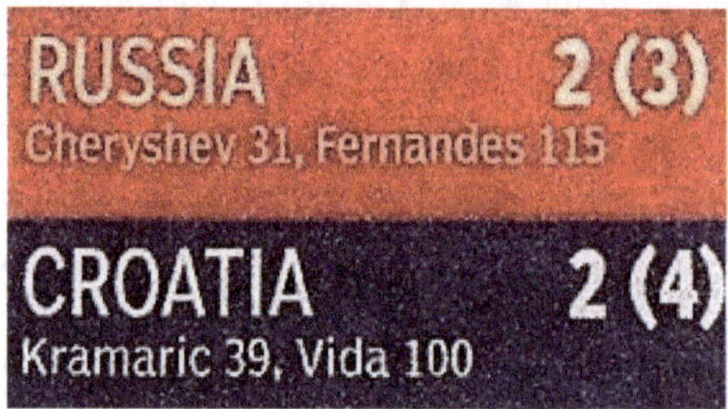

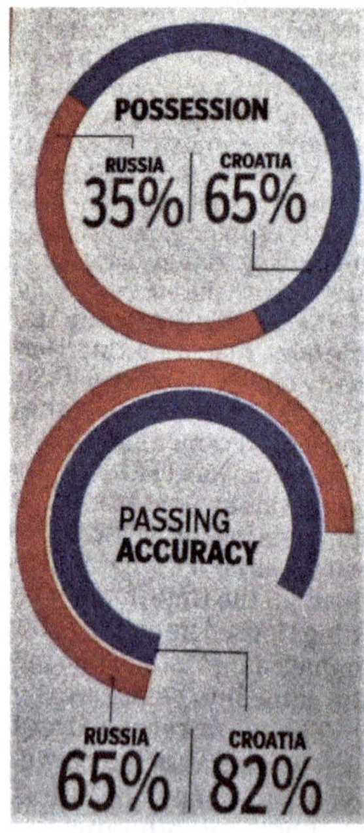

MATCH STATS

RUSSIA		CROATIA
13	Total Shots	18
5	Shots on Target	3
6	Corners	8
400	Total Passes	730
18	Total Crosses	38
77	Balls Recovered	89
1	Yellow Cards	4
25	Fouls Committed	18

PENALTY SHOOTOUT

RUSSIA	CROATIA
Smolov	Brozovic
Dzagoev	Kovacic
Fernandes	Modric
Ignashevich	Vida
Kuziaev	Rakitic

Russia salutes heroes after the dream run ends.

The Kremlin dubbed the Russian national team heroes, and proud football fans saluted their underdog host team after the side lost on penalties to Croatia, Bringing an end to its World Cup challenge at the quarterfinals. "Our boys, they really did great. A huge thank you to them for this tournament. What we achieved was so cool," Andrey, a lawyer, said next to the street corner screen that had shown the match. President Vladimir Putin did not attend the game. Still, he watched remotely, saying the players were heroes despite the defeat and the country was proud of them.

TEAMS QUALIFIED FOR SEMI-FINALS

1. FRANCE
2. BELGIUM
3. CROATIA
4. ENGLAND

SEMI-FINALS

FRANCE
FIFA RANKING: 7

ROAD TO SEMIS:
(Group stage) Beat Australia 2-1, Beat Peru 1-0, Drew with Denmark 0-0; (Round of 16) Beat Argentina 4-3; (Quarterfinal) Beat Uruguay 2-0
Top goalscorer: Kylian Mbappe & Antoine Griezmann (3 goals each)
Missing: All available.
While they have never really looked troubled until now, France have come across to many as a side that's still not playing to its true potential. Will they finally explode into life against Belgium?

KYLIAN MBAPPE

3 GOALS

COACH
Didier Deschamps

VS

BELGIUM
FIFA RANKING: 3

ROAD TO SEMIS:
(Group stage) Beat Panama 3-0, Beat Tunisia 5-2, Beat England 1-0; (Round of 16) Beat Japan 3-2; (Quarterfinal) Beat Brazil 2-1
Top goalscorer: Romelu Lukaku (4 goals)
Missing: Right back Thomas Meunier through suspension.
A combination of grit and ruthlessness helped them script a famous 2-1 win over Brazil in the quarterfinals but Eden Hazard and company can expect another fierce battle against France.

ROMELU LUKAKU

4 GOALS

COACH
Roberto Martinez

CROATIA
FIFA RANKING: 20

ROAD TO SEMIS:
(Group stage) Beat Nigeria 2-0, Beat Argentina 3-0, Beat Iceland 2-1; (Round of 16) Beat Denmark 3-2 on penalties, match ended 1-1 after extra time; (Quarterfinal) Beat Russia 4-3 on penalties, match ended 2-2 after extra time
Top goalscorer: Luka Modric (2 goals)
Missing: All available.
Modric and mates are a win away from going further than their 1998 compatriots. However, they have put in a lot of hours with both their knockouts going the distance.

LUKA MODRIC

2 GOALS

COACH
Zlatko Dalic

VS

ENGLAND
FIFA RANKING: 12

ROAD TO SEMIS:
(Group stage) Beat Tunisia 2-1, Beat Panama 6-1, Lost to Belgium 1-0; (Round of 16) Beat Colombia 4-3 on penalties, match ended 1-1 after extra time; (Quarterfinal) Beat Sweden 2-0
Top goalscorer: Harry Kane (6 goals)
Missing: All available.
In reaching the semifinals, Southgate's side are already being hailed as heroes for accomplishing what no England team has managed since 1990. Croatia, though, may just prove to be their sternest test yet.

HARRY KANE

6 GOALS

COACH
Gareth Southgate

'FRANCE FAVOURITE TO WIN WORLD CUP'

TOI ONLINE POLL
Over 91,000 responses

1 Who will win the World Cup?
Belgium 29%, France 44%, England 18%, Croatia 9%

2 Which team deserved to be in the semifinal line-up?
Brazil 49% | Spain 21% | Germany 17% | Argentina 13%

3 Who was the biggest flop of the World Cup?
Messi 65%

Over 97% respondents gave thumbs up to VAR (Video Assisted Referee)

(Figures till Monday, 2 pm)

French midfielder Pogba and forward Giroud (on top)

Two intriguing semifinals lie ahead. The first is between the upwardly mobile Belgium and the pedigreed France. Both sides are on top of their game. A mouthwatering contest, certainly. Then there's England, closer to their dreams of a second World Cup triumph, clashing with the formidable Croatia, the only east European team left in World Cup 2018. Don't miss either of the matches. Nail-biters are the flavour of the season

Tintin vs Asterix | Class vs Class

Belgium vs France | July 10, 11.30pm St Petersburg

WHAT TO EXPECT
A crackling attacking game with plenty of openings created by either side

Belgium

Rank 3 | Nickname: Les Diables Rouges (The Red Devils) | WC Best 4th in 1986

France

Rank 7 | Nickname: Les Bleus (The Blues) | WC Best Winners, 1998

Strengths & Weaknesses:
In top gear. The midfield is muscular. Fellaini's towering presence also offers aerial power. The Red Devils have the pace and inventiveness of Hazard, De Bruyne and Lukaku upfront. But Belgium's tactically astute coach, Spaniard Roberto Martinez, will miss suspended defender Meunier's reassuring presence. Also aging defender Kompany is susceptible to errors, though goalie Courtois is back at his best.

Coach: Roberto Martinez

TOI Poser: Will Martinez use the same attacking formation as against Brazil?

Fellaini

Strengths & Weaknesses:
Oozing pedigree and star power. Mbappe is the hottest young star in the game. Kante is the team's preventive medicine for any possible ailments in the midfield. Pogba has shown class in winning tackles. Central defender Varane is in top form both in defence and offence, heading in the opening goal against Uruguay. Overall, solid all-round team with no evident weakness. However, statistics show that the forward line needs to be more proactive. And it's true that Griezmann, the 27-year-old striker, is yet to hit peak form

Coach: Didier Deschamps

TOI Poser: Can Deschamps' team attack more and hustle Belgium's leaky defence?

Griezmann

When Harry Meets Luka | Punisher vs Playmaker

England vs Croatia | July 11, 11.30pm Moscow

WHAT TO EXPECT
A close encounter of the intense kind, where set-pieces will be vital

England

Rank 12 | Nickname: The Three Lions | WC Best Winners, 1966

Croatia

Rank 20 | Nickname: Vatreni (The Blazers) | WC Best 3rd in 1998

Strengths & Weaknesses:
Scoring goals off set-pieces, three so far, has been among the biggest strengths of Southgate's side. His England is young and fearless, playing with a rare freedom and abandon. Trippier has excelled as a multi-purpose defender. Henderson holds the midfield together. Kane is able upfront and Sterling has dribbled past defenders at will. If only, he knew how to score.

Coach: Gareth Southgate

TOI Poser: Can this young team handle the biggest night of their lives, as England chants "it's coming home"?

FOR MORE WORLD CUP THRILLS AND SPILLS, TURN TO THE OTHER SIDE OF THIS PAGE

Henderson

Vida

Strengths & Weaknesses:
Croatia have the championship's best-performing player: Modric. From releasing crossfield passes to dribbling past defenders, from unleashing long rangers to shielding the ball, the Real Madrid star has done it all. Then there's Ivan Rakitic, the extremely efficient defensive medio and master of earning free-kicks. The Croats have a strong back four including the persevering Lovren and powerful Vida. The frontline lacks the finesse of a Hazard but both Perisic and Mandzukic are hardworking and can do the job

Coach: Zlatko Dalic

TOI Poser: Can they finish this crunch knocko[ut] game without going to penalties?

IN NUMBERS: THE FAB FOUR Performance

Most goals scored Belgium: 14
Least goals scored France: 9
Most shots at goal Belgium: 85
Most goals conceded Belgium: 5
Least goals conceded England, Croatia, France: 4
Least shots at goal France: 56
Most fouls committed Croatia: 78
Least fouls committed England: 53
Maximum yellow cards Croatia: 12
Most fouls suffered Croatia: 80
Least fouls suffered Belgium: 64
Least yellow cards England: 5

Beastly Tales

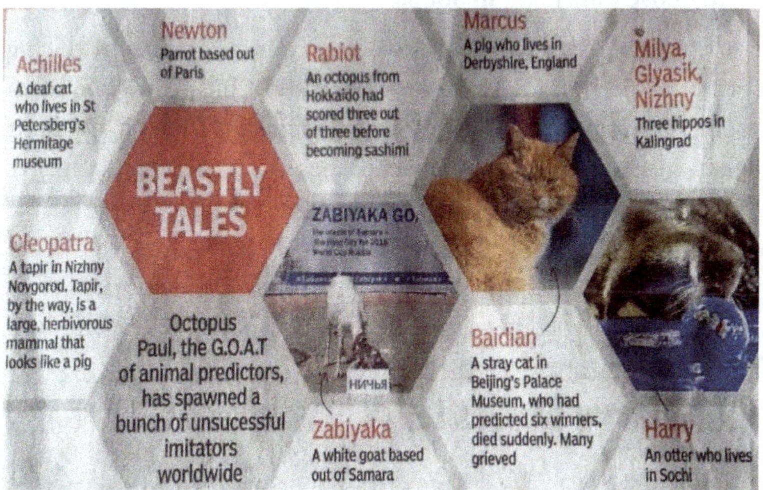

There'd be no World Cup for them without their parent's sacrifices.

To go with the Golden Boot for the World Cup's top scorer and the best player's golden ball, tournament organiser FIFA should consider a new award, a Golden steering wheel. That prize could be for all the parents and mentors who schlepped in all types of whether to Heaven knows how many practices and made all kinds of other sacrifices so soccer-obsessed kids could grow up to become the stars who are now within touching distance of the Sport most coveted trophy. It could, for example, go to the mother of Raheem Sterling, the forward to whom all of England will be looking for defence-shredding dribbles in the semi-final against Croatia. After the murder of his father when Sterling was at the age of two, his mother put herself through school and worked as a hotel cleaner. Other potential award candidates are Alain and Isabelle, Griezmann's parents, and Benjamin Pavard's parents, Frederic and Nathalie.

Cat Luck for Croatia

Croatia Love Puts Joker in Soup.

Serbian tennis player Novak Djokovic has come under fire for voicing support for neighbours Croatia at the World Cup. "Only idiots can support Croatia. Aren't you ashamed, Novak?" Tweeted Vladimir Djukanovic of President Aleksander Vucic's ruling Serbian Progressive party. "I am backing Croatia... I know who I would like to lift the trophy," Inverted Serbian media quoted Djokovic as saying from Wimbledon. Prior to the World Cup, Djokovic posted pictures of himself with Croatian players, including stars Luka Modric and Ivan Rakitic.

FRANCE VS BELGIUM

STADIUM - SAINT PETERSBURG

MATCH STATS

FRANCE		BELGIUM
19	Total Shots	9
5	Shots on Target	3
4	Corners	5
345	Total Passes	594
11	Total Crosses	26
50	Balls Recovered	43
2	Yellow Cards	3
6	Fouls Committed	16

3 Number of finals France have reached since playing their first title clash in 1998 – more than any other nation.

1 This was Belgium's first defeat of any kind since a friendly loss against Spain in September 2016.

20 Goals Antoine Griezmann has been directly involved in his last 20 competitive games for France (12 goals, 8 assists).

13 Shots France's Olivier Giroud has had in the 2018 World Cup, with none of them on target. Since 1966, no player has had more attempts in a single tournament without getting one on target.

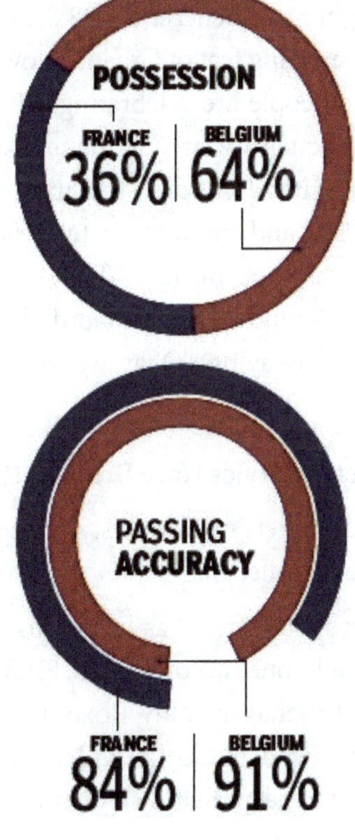

ENGLAND VS CROATIA

STADIUM - LUZHNIKI STADIUM

Show more respect: Modric to English Media.

Luka Modric was struggling to express his feelings after leading his team to a historic win. "It's very difficult to find words to express how I feel right now. Generation '98 finished third in France, and it was the biggest sporting feat of Croatia. Now we have overtaken them. Look at how the people are celebrating," the Croatian captain said. "A lot of heart and quality went into the semi-finals victory against England, but what has irked Modric the most is the lack of respect." English journalists, and pundits on television, underestimated Croatia, and that was a huge mistake. They should be humble and respect the opponent's mode. All these words from them we take, we were reading, and we were saying, "Okay, we will see today who will be tired."

A Variety of Styles Have Brought the World Cup in Russia to Life

The wide variety of playing styles employed by the 32 teams at the why, plus the so-called.

Guardiola's effect has helped to make the tournament in Russia a memorable one, according to FIFA's technical study group. Former Scotland manager Andy Roxburgh One of a number of prominent exporters who made the video, said that individual countries still managed to keep their own distinctive playing style even though most players are best with European clubs.

THIRD-PLACE PLAY-OFF

BELGIUM VS ENGLAND

STADIUM - SAINT PETERSBURG

Bronze For Belgium's 'Golden Generation

Belgium beat England 2 – 0 in the World Cup third-place play-off to secure their best-ever finish at the World Cup and send Gareth Southgate's side home with a second straight loss. A fourth-minute goal from Thomas Meunier and an 82nd-minute goal by Eden Hazard strike earned Belgium the victory and third place, which improves on their previous best performance of a fourth-place finish in 1986. "It is all about that achievement. I think these players deserve that." Said Belgium coach Roberto Martinez. England was on top for most of the second half, but with captain, Harry Kane looking tired, Belgium's greater sharpness in the match proved decisive. Belgium's early strike came when Romelu Lukaku swung the ball out left to Nacer Chadli, who burst down the wing and slipped the ball across the face of the goal, and Meunier confidently slotted past Jordan pick sold. The goal means Belgium has had 10 different goal scorers at this World Cup, equalling the record set by France in 1982 and Italy in 2006. England nearly equalised when Eric Dier got cleared and chipped over Thibaut Courtois, only for Toby Alderweireld to make a sliding clearance off the line. Belgium finished off the game when Kevin De Bruyne set Hazard clear and swept his shot past goalkeeper Jordan Pickford.

WORLD CUP FINAL

Spotlight On Penalties

Penalty kicks have been a major talking point at this edition, with a record number of 28 awarded. 21 of the 28 were converted. The introduction of VAR played a role in this, with 10 of the spot kicks awarded after reviews. Here is a graphical representation of the penalty kicks, excluding shootouts.

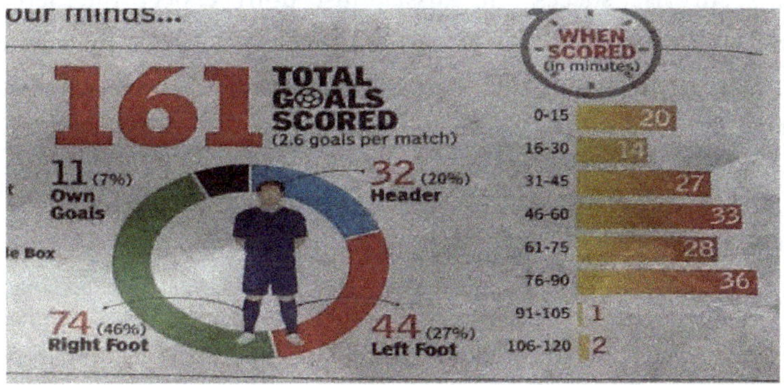

Argentina's Former Actor Pitana to Referee World Cup Final

Nestor Pitana of Argentina will referee the World Cup final between France and Croatia, FIFA announced. Pitana, A former actor who has already refereed four games, including the tournament opener between host nation Russia and Saudi Arabia and France's quarterfinal win over Uruguay, will take charge of the World Cup in Russia.

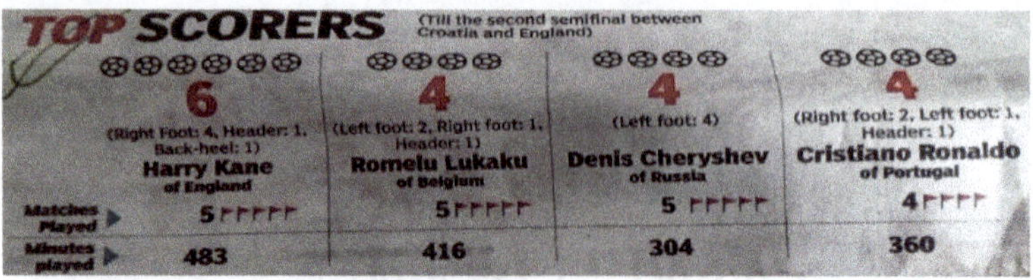

Success divides Balkan Neighbours

Croatia's neighbours in the former Yugoslavia have largely praised the team's surprise success in Russia; just don't expect the Serbian President to support them, at least for now. Every time a tournament comes around, a familiar refrain is heard in the region: "If only Yugoslavia was one country, imagine the amazing team we could have."

Their cup is full:

Javier Mascherano, 34 (Argentina)

It was a forgettable farewell for El Jefecito ('The little chief'), who now plies his trade in the Chinese league. The 34-year-old's legs just could not handle the flurry of the young Frenchmen in the round of 16. Still, the figure of a bloodied Mascherano with his diminishing powers was not the most impressive image we were left with before his superannuation.

Andres Iniesta, 34 (Spain)

It has been a trip down memory lane for the midfield metronome. The

World Cup was not meant to be, as Spain's Tiki-Taka failed to make inroads into a determined and direct Russian team. Iniesta's name was missing from the starting line-up, and when he came on, perhaps the writing was on the wall. Hark back to 2010, and the cup-winning goal in extra time against the Dutch, and the celebratory tribute to Dani Jarque. "The hardest thing is to make it look effortless, and that's Andres," Messi said.

Edinson Cavani and Luis Suarez, 31 (Uruguay)

Both strikes will be 35 by the time Qatar 2022 comes around, and there is a likelihood that they may not be around to guide Uruguay to the finals. Although the abiding images of Suarez are negative, the blatant handball saves against Ghana and a chunk of Chiellini's shoulder, his bulldozing presence has always been a threat to the opposition. The net-bulging effect of the Suarez and Cavani combo was there for all to see in Sochi, and the latter was greatly missed in the quarters against France.

Cristiano Ronaldo, 33 (Portugal) & Lionel Messi, 31 (Argentina)

The GOAT debate continues as Ronaldo and Messi's lives are destined to be entwined. Leaving Russia on the same night may have been the final subplot of their World Cup careers, but you never know. While part of the script will change as Ronaldo heads to Serie A to detach strings with La Liga's Messi, people will always find a way to link the two superstars. Ronaldo claims he is 33 going on 24, while Messi has deferred his decision regarding his international career. We will have to wait and see. A four-year cycle can be a long time.

WORLD CUP FINAL

FRANCE VS CROATIA

STADIUM - LUZHNIKI STADIUM

FRANCE FULL SQUAD

GOALKEEPERS: HUGO LLORIS, STEVE MANDANDA, ALPHONSE AREOLA

DEFENDERS: DJIBRIL SIDIBE, BENJAMIN PAVARD, ADIL RAMI, RAPHAEL VARANE, SAMUEL UMTITI, PRESNEL KIMPEMBE, BENJAMIN MENDY, LUCAS HERNANDEZ

MIDFIELDERS: PAUL POGBA, BLAISE MATUIDI, CORENTIN TOLISSO, N'GOLO KANTE, STEVEN NZONZI

FORWARDS: KYLIAN MBAPPE, OLIVIER GIROUD, ANTOINE GRIEZMANN, OUSMAN DEMBELE, FLORIAN THAUVIN, THOMAS LEMAR, NABIL FEKIR

CROATIA FULL SQUAD

GOALKEEPERS: DANIJEL SUBASIC, LOVRE KALINIC, DOMINIK LIVAKOVIC

DEFENDERS: VEDRAN CORLUKA, DOMAGOJ VIDA, IVAN STRINIC, DEJAN LOVREN, SIME VRSALJKO, JOSIP PIVARIC, TIN JEDVAJ, DUJE CALETA - CAR.

MIDFIELDERS: LUKA MODRIC, IVAN RAKITIC, MATEO KOVACIC, MILAN BADELJ, MARCELO BROZOVIC, FILIP BRADARIC

FORWARDS: MARIO MANDZUKIC, IVAN PERISIC, NIKOLA KALINIC, ANDREJ KRAMARIC, MARKO PJACA, ANTE REBIC

THE WORLD IS BLEUS

The run of the underdogs came to an end at the Luzhniki Stadium. Drenched by sudden showers towards the end. Luka Modric's Croatia lost steam after a fighting first half. It failed to stop the French Revolution engineered by French coach Didier Deschamps and his rainbow team. Till their legs could carry them, Croatia fought to pin down the likes of Paul Pogba, Blaise Matuidi, and N'golo Kante into their own half. Once Fatigue set in, luck, too, stopped smiling on the Croatian brave hearts. As Pogba found his gear, Croatian resistance melted away, and France wrapped up their second World Cup 4–2 in a deserving fashion. With the half-time score 2–1, Croatia still harboured hopes of a comeback, and they were successful in cutting the communication lines between Pogba and Kylian Mbappe till the 59th minute.

French fans go wild, from Paris to Moscow.

Millions of French football fans were delirious with joy as France beat Croatia 4 – 2 in the FIFA World Cup in a pulsating final in Moscow that sparked ecstatic scenes from Paris to Marseille and beyond. In Paris, where 90,000 people gathered next to the Eiffel Tower to watch the match on vast TV screens, there were choruses of the Marseillaise honking horns and hundreds and thousands of red, white, and blue French flags fluttering in the breeze. The boom of fireworks and firecrackers filled the air, and car drivers honked their horns incessantly to celebrate France's second World Cup title after their triumph on home soil in 1998. A deafening chorus of 'We are the champions' rang out from the Sacre Coeur in the north of the city to the Sorbonne on the left bank.

MATCH **STATS**

FRANCE		CROATIA
7	Total Shots	14
6	Shots on Target	4
2	Corners	6
285	Total Passes	529
5	Total Crosses	28
61	Balls Recovered	69
2	Yellow Cards	1
13	Fouls Committed	13

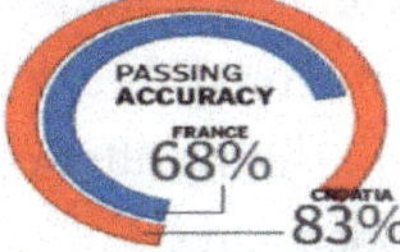

We have no regrets because we were the better team for much of the game. Some clumsy goals swung it their way... but we can hold our heads high.

—Luka Modric

I don't know where I am, it is great... Very happy. It was a difficult match. Croatia played a great game. We started timidly. We knew it was a World Cup Final. We got into the game and on counter attacks, we made the difference."

—Antoine Griezmann

Only the second teenager to have scored a goal in a #WorldCupFinal! Welcome to the club, @KMbappe - it's great to have some company!

—Pele

World Cup in Records:

As one of the most entertaining World Cups ends, here is a look at some of the records created and broken during the tournament:

Plenty of Goals

With just 1 goalless draw in 64 matches, this World Cup was far from dull. The tournament averaged 2.6 goals per game, second only to Brazil in 2014 for World Cups this century. The record of 5.38 per game from 1954 is unlikely to be ever broken.

Own Goals

Teams have scored more goals than usual, but many weren't particularly noteworthy. The 12 own goals are a record, in part because FIFA has stricter guidelines about attributing deflected shots.

More Penalties

The new Video Assistant Referee (V.A.R.) system led to an increase in the number of penalties awarded to a record 29, 11 more than the previous mark from 2002. Of those, 22 were converted from the spot. Harry Kane typified the trend in his push to be the tournament's top scorer. The England captain scored three of his tournament-leading goals from penalties and two shortly after corner kicks, leaving just a single deflected goal from open play.

The Young and the Old

Young stars have made a mark none more than France's 19-year-old Kylian Mbappe, who became the youngest player to score two goals in a World Cup since Pele in 1958. Ageing players have set records too. Egypt's goalkeeper Essam El Haddary became the oldest player to ever start in a World Cup.

Extra - Time = Extra - Grit

Croatia got to the final the hard way, becoming the first team ever to win three consecutive games in extra time at a World Cup. That added up to 360 minutes of football in the knockout stages.

Less Red Cards

Perhaps with one eye on the VAR system, players didn't break the rules so much. There hasn't been a single red card for violent conduct, and just four ejections in total. If it stays that way, it'll be the lowest number at the World Cup for 40 years.

TOTAL GOALS

TOTAL GOALS | 169

6 Harry Kane (England)

4 Kylian Mbappe (France), Antoine Griezmann (France), Romelu Lukaku (Belgium), Denis Cheryshev (Russia), Cristiano Ronaldo (Portugal)

3 Costa (ESP), Cavani (URU), Dzyuba (RUS), Mina (COL), Perisic (CRO), Mandzukic (CRO), Hazard (BEL)

2 Jedinak (AUS), Modric (CRO), Coutinho (BRA), Musa (NIG), Stones (ENG), Suarez (URU), Salah (EGY), Son (S KOR), Granqvist (SWE), Khazri (TUN), Aguero (ARG), Neymar (BRA), Inui (JPN)

1: 84 players have a goal each

UPDATED AFTER WC FINAL

own goals 12

HOW THE CUP WAS WON

GROUP STAGE

June 16	France beat Australia 2-1
June 21	France beat Peru 1-0
June 26	France 0 Denmark 0

ROUND OF 16

June 30	France beat Argentina 4-3

QUARTERFINAL

July 6	France beat Uruguay 2-0

SEMIFINAL

July 10	France beat Belgium 1-0

FINAL

July 15	France beat Croatia 4-2

WORLD CUP FINAL GOAL-FESTS

This World Cup final was the first to witness four or more goals after the 1986 edition. A look at other goal-fests in finals

1930	Uruguay 4 Argentina 2
1938	Italy 4 Hungary 2
1954	West Germany 3 Hungary 2
1958	Brazil 5 Sweden 2
1962	Brazil 3 Czhechoslovakia 1
1966	England 4 West Germany 2
1970	Brazil 4 Italy 1
1978	Argentina 3 Netherlands 1
1982	Italy 3 West Germany 1
1986	Argentina 3 West Germany 2
2018	France 4 Croatia 2

INDIVIDUAL AWARDS

Golden Ball: Luka Modric (CRO)
Golden Boot: Harry Kane (ENG) – 6 goals
Golden Glove: Thibaut Courtois (BEL)
Young Player: Kylian Mbappe (FRA)

DASVIDANIYA

I am earnestly thankful for the newspaper Times of India and a few other journals from where I was encouraged, and which enabled me to complete this project by providing me with the feed material.

– *Author*

ABOUT THE AUTHOR

Gunnmay is an extraordinary child prodigy who has captured the hearts and minds of many with his exceptional talents and passion for various fields. Despite their young age, Gunnmay has already achieved remarkable success in academics, writing, sports, particularly soccer, and has shown a strong commitment to environmentalism. He is a remarkable young talent who is making waves far beyond their years & has already managed to capture the attention and admiration of several stalwarts.

Gunnmay demonstrates an insatiable appetite for knowledge, consistently achieving top grades in school impressing teachers and peers alike. He is a remarkable child prodigy who has consistently excelled in academics since an early age. Participated in various competitions and won several awards. Being charmed by trivia & figures further enthused Gunnmay into writing.

At the tender age of 8, Gunnmay already displayed remarkable writing skills. His literary talents have been acknowledged through numerous awards and accolades, including local writing competitions and regional events. He has a natural storytelling ability and a gift for crafting captivating narratives that resonate with readers of all ages. Authored several short stories and poems that have been recognized and published in various journals and magazines. Truly a budding literary sensation who has been able to make connects with experts and audience alike.

Gunnmay is a star Vlogger of his generation who has the credit of being recognized as the "Youngest Gardener" who is successfully running an Organic home gardening YouTube channel and Facebook page by the name—"My Urban Organic Garden" which has a loyal fan following. He has been invited as a participant in the Protect Our Planet India Seminar led by Dr. R.K. Pachauri. He was a participant in a Global Seminar on climate change hosted by India Today and sponsored by several corporates Gunnmay was the only child activist participant. He has also raised the issue of including Horticulture in the non-scholastic curriculum of schools in India with the Prime Minister of India, Shri Narendra Modi.

We love creating beautiful books for you!

Come be a part of our ever-growing community of authors. Grow, write, and publish with us!

Scan here to explore
books, authors and more

Connect with us on socials. We'd love to hear from you!

    Inkfeathers Publishing

www.ingramcontent.com/pod-product-compliance
Lightning Source LLC
LaVergne TN
LVHW052008160826
845678LV00005B/1680

* 9 7 8 8 1 1 9 4 8 3 5 1 8 *